Aldo Aymonino, Valerio Paolo Mosco

Contemporary Public Space
Un-volumetric Architecture

Cover
Ira Koers, Jurjen Zeinstra,
Mikel van Gelderen, *Slijtplein*
Helsinki University, *Kupla – The Bubble:
Korkeasaari Zoo Lookout Tower*
Luis Barragán, *Fuentes de Los Amantes*
Studio Granda, *Kringlumyra Bridge*
Zaha Hadid Architects, *Terminus multimodal
Hoenheim Nord*
Cooperativa Amereida, *Ciudad abierta*
Frederic Schwartz Architects, *The Hoboken
September 11th Memorial*

Back cover
Gerry Judah, *Renault Central Display*

Editor
Luca Molinari

Design
Marcello Francone

Editing
Marta Cattaneo
Francesca Ruggiero

Layout
Paola Ranzini

Translations
Christopher Huw Evans
Laura Mejier
Leslie Ray

First published in Italy in 2006
by Skira Editore S.p.A.
Palazzo Casati Stampa
via Torino 61
20123 Milano
Italy
www.skira.net

© 2006 by Skira editore
© Luis Barragán, Christian de Portzamparc,
Lucien Den Arend, Dominique Perrault,
Hannu Siren, Saul Steinberg, by SIAE 2006
© Fondation Le Corbusier, by SIAE 2006

Printed and bound in Italy. First edition

ISBN-13: 978-88-7624-273-1
ISBN-10: 88-7624-273-2

Distributed in North America by Rizzoli
International Publications, Inc., 300 Park
Avenue South, New York, NY 10010.
Distributed elsewhere in the world by
Thames and Hudson Ltd., 181a High
Holborn, London WC1V 7QX, United
Kingdom.

Thanks
To Denise Scott-Brown, without whose
advice and encouragement this book
would not have been possible.
To Luca Molinari, friend and last
hope.
To George Hascup, with whom we
devised the term "un-volumetric
architecture".

To all those who dedicated their
energies enthusiastically to writing
the essays.

I
- - -
U
- - -
A
- - -
V

To the IUAV in Venice and specifically
Marino Folin, Carlo Magnani and
Giancarlo Carnevale and the secretary
of the Planning Department.

And to the people who supervised the
completion of the book: Livia La
Terza, Tecla Mazzarella and Valentina
Lancerin.

And also to the Municipality of
Gibellina, Federica Zanco of the
Barragán Foundation, the Pomodoro
Foundation, the Le Corbusier
Foundation and the photographic
archives of Casabella.

Where not specified otherwise, the
texts are by Valerio Paolo Mosco.

Contents

Foreword
Denise Scott Brown

Louis I. Kahn defined architecture as "the thoughtful making of space." This was an attractive proposition in the 1960s because, at a time when all qualitative definitions were under reappraisal, it set intentionality as the basis of the definition. This meant that the possibility of "bad" as well as "good" architecture was included. But in his formulation Kahn took for granted that architecture's main task was the making of space. In the 1960s this was not questioned. Yet in the late 1940s, I had been taught that architecture had to do with mass and volume. Space came in the 1950s. Now we see, in this book, the suggestion that architecture can exist without volume.

Earlier theorists seem to have skirted the issue. Vitruvius, for example, defined architecture by listing three of its abstract qualities — strength, utility and beauty. In the eighteenth century, Laugier imagined architecture's origins in a rustic, twiggy structure, built by primordial tribes, but idealized in his version through the lens of Romanticism. In the 1950s, the architectural historian, Reyner Banham, suggested that primitive living arrangements could be non-volumetric —that in some climates, nature could be manipulated through campfires to provide all the shelter needed. Banham likened this to the tempering of the environment in our day by mechanical systems. At the other end of the spectrum was the cave, a found accommodation that protects and shelters. And between these, we might insert Laugier-like structures, erected expediently perhaps by nomads, out of whatever was to hand —twigs and branches, but also skins or blocks of ice.

Some non-volumetric categories in this book —canopies, skin structures, and technological and micro-structures— seem to originate conceptually with the skins and branches of the primitive hut. They go back, too, to early Modern architects' fascination with Constructivism and transparency, and to 1950s experiments with thin-slab and lightweight frame structures, made under the influence of engineers. With elaborate sarcasm, Buckminster Fuller once asked, "Madam, how much does your house weigh?"

Post World War II architects associated structural lightness with technical efficiency but, in our experience, lightness creates problems in architecture. For one thing, it is vulnerable to the erosions of weather and use. In campus planning, we find that the construction dates of existing buildings often indicate which are candidates for demolition, owing to wear, tear and lack of adaptability. Many turn out to be from the 1950s and 1960s. Buildings built before them are frequently sturdier and last longer. From this we've concluded that most buildings of a society need to sit foursquare on the ground, supported by relatively sturdy structures and set within their own, relatively heavy skins; and that a degree of weight and mass will help with environmental management, climate control, sustainability, maintenance, and lifetime costs.

However, despite our skepticism about lightweight structures, the concept of non-volumetric architecture became important to us through our studies of Las Vegas in the 1960s. This urbanism —so different from Las Vegas today— was dominated, not by buildings, but by signs.

In a general way, desert buildings face the quandary that they are small relative to the vast space around them. A solution as old as Karnak was to project lines across the vastness: sightlines, defined by points of various kinds, set in the desert. At Karnak the points were rows of crouched lions. They helped to modulate the approach and direct the view to the relatively small Temple of Khons.

In the 1960s, Las Vegas followed this example. The scale of the Mojave Desert and of the desert of parked cars on the Strip swamped even the largest casinos. Their walls could not define the boundaries of the street. As at Karnak, space had to be modulated by vistas projected across it. The "points" that marked the vistas were signs, large and small. Their function was to communicate with people driving and riding, giving them messages about casino hotels and other establishments set back from the Strip.

On the 1960s Las Vegas Strip the signs were much more prominent than the buildings. They were what was seen first. Their high readers guided visitors to the buildings, then their low readers gave information on events to be found inside. Approaching Las Vegas, one understood (as in any city) that density was increasing as one neared the center. But here the perception had to do, not with the larger size and closer spacing of buildings, but with a greater intensity in the rhythm of communication. This was a non-spatial, non-volumetric form of definition, far from that of the traditional city.

Planned as carefully as scientific equipment, these neon giants were visible from the air. They inspired our slogan: "Symbol in Space Before Form in Space." And in the process of marking and advertising private buildings, they defined the public identity, formal and symbolic of the Strip and, to a considerable extent, of the city.

But although a neon sign might be 22 stories high and emit an overwhelming intensity of illumination, the mark representing it on a land-use map or urban design plan was scarcely visible. In our "Learning from Las Vegas" studio we considered how the non-volumetric urbanism of signs should be documented, given the failures of both land-use mapping and orthographic projection to show its importance in the city.

The thinness yet strength of the signs gave rise, as well, to thought on the geometry of ornament. Baroque decoration needed a depth of one meter to express itself. Classical decoration and that of antiquity, perhaps 20 centimeters. Rococo frizzled up to a couple of centimeters, and so did the bas-relief of Art Deco, which could suggest seven or eight different layers of space in a centimeter or two. We found Deco

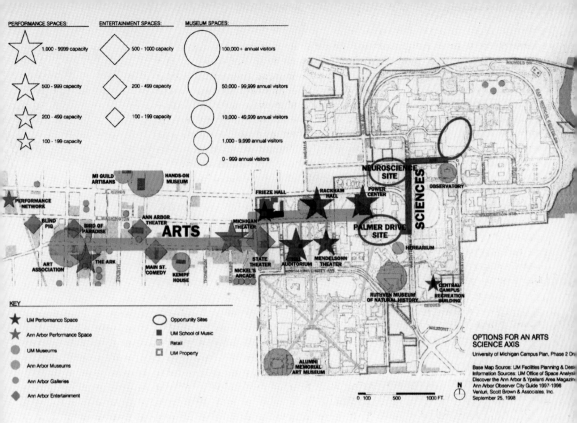

University of Michigan
Campus plan, Venturi, Scott
Brown and Associates,
1998

low relief especially intriguing and sympathetic to our concerns, yet, as we considered ways to do decorative communication and allusion for our time, we began to realize that even this relief was not low enough. The shallower the decoration, the nearer its depth to zero, the more in line would it be with the requirements of building economics and urban communication in our time. Indeed, the ultimate could be light-emitting diodes, which have breadth and height but no depth. So our most recent interpretation of the Decorated Shed is that the shed has volume, but the decoration is LED and has surface only.

Another non-volumetric order of architecture is "spatial" form, as defined by regional scientists and urban economists. For them, "spatial organization" concerns two-dimensional patterns of land settlement and the factors that determine them —travel time and costs; locations of markets or raw materials; and labor, land, and other costs. We've found a knowledge of the patterns of regional science useful in understanding the relation between the buildings we are designing and their broader environment.

In urban and campus design and planning, spatial patterns can be analyzed and synthesized in various ways. They can be disaggregated then rejuxtaposed to highlight connections important to design. For example, the locations and sizes of all classroom spaces on campus can be mapped and these can be shown in relation to volumes of pedestrian circulation, or to stores and eating-places in the city near the campus. Although a vertical dimension —upper floor uses— should be included in land use studies, the patterns are still non-volumetric. They merely stack up. Yet they can also be seen as pre-volumetric, because out of them architecture can be evolved.

We have used economic spatial planning and urban land-use and transportation planning as tools, not only for the planning of cities and campuses, but also for the design of buildings. They offer means of considering volumetric architecture non-volumetrically: of studying the relations desired among the activities to be housed and devising patterns of use, access and circulation to achieve them. This involves seeing buildings as answering to the same laws of gravity and potential —the same "urban physics"— that connect levels of access and density of development in cities.

For me, the patterns created by urban systems are more basic to urban design than is *arredamento urbano*, "urban furnishing." I feel spatial organization, in the economic sense, should be understood by architects for the richness it can add to design in three dimensions. Then buildings will have land use and transportation plans on the inside, and also "100% areas," where major corridors and vertical circulation —"main streets"— meet and where facilities needed by everyone are located.

But there's as well the possibility of four-dimensional architecture, which takes time into account and considers how the uses of a building may change over the years. And conceptually there could be n-dimensional space which, for architects involved with the concrete, is difficult to conceive. In addition, we should include non-volumetric architecture from various climates and environments, whose buildings are produced under cultural and technological assumptions different from those of Europe or the US, and whose landscapes are viewed through a diversity of interpretive lenses.

By enlarging architecture's scope and conceptual categories, by accepting that our field is involved in both more and less than the making of space, this book can bring new dimensions and added richness to what we do.

Introduction
More space, less volume: a story in movement
Aldo Aymonino

"We get to know reality by changing it." (Karl Marx)

This book stems from a reflection on the interpretation of a number of architectural and spatial phenomena that are changing some of the fundamental and structural concepts (and preconceptions) of the discipline of architecture in a radical and pervasive way, a fact with which everyone by now is essentially in agreement.

If from the middle of the 1910s to the end of the 1980s a ferment of ideas had taken shape around studies of the city, of its construction, its growth and its more macroscopic and recurrent phenomena, there can be no doubt that since the 1990s attention has shifted, in an apparently abrupt manner, to territory and landscape.

These new and still evolving perspectives have been introduced not so much by those who, by the articles of their profession, devote themselves to study and planning on a territorial scale. Principally they have come from architects and from researchers and experts in "other" disciplines (anthropologists, sociologists, geographers, critics, photographers, etc.) who, starting out from observation of the changes underway and through the interaction between different cultures, have succeeded in indicating lines of research capable of attracting growing interest, as well as funding and resources.

On closer examination, however, the first sporadic attempts at a systematic approach were made, with different effects and repercussions on European and American architectural culture, as far back as the sixties. This was when books and research papers began to be published on both sides of the Atlantic that no longer focused exclusively on the form and possible evolution of the city, but on other factors affecting the anthropic environment (systems connected with the infrastructure, environment, landscape, reclamation, energy conservation, etc.): phenomena that had previously been considered ancillary with respect to the central core of the discipline, consisting, as has been said, exclusively of the study of the modes of sedimentation and development of the urban form.

In this sense, to take two examples from urban cultures as profoundly different in their critical approach and methodology at the time as those of the United States and Italy, it suffices to think of Appleyard, Lynch and Myer's *The View from the Road*, published in 1964, and the monographic issue of *Edilizia Moderna* in 1966, edited by Gregotti and devoted to the "Form of the Territory" in order to see how, as early as four decades ago, an oblique and indirect gaze connected apparently incompatible territories and social objectives.

In more or less the same period even studies of the city underwent some profound epistemological shake-ups. On the American continent (but elsewhere too) this was due to the slippery transmutation of the *forma urbis*, which was no longer able to throw any light on the age-old (and now pointless) question of "where does the city end?". A question that increasingly often received bureaucratic, consolatory and imprecise answers.

It was realized, in fact, that a rapid shift was taking place from an idea of city-territory (in which the city, transformed in the meantime into a metropolis, maintained and expanded its role as a catalyst of the surrounding territory) to one of territory-city (where the isotropic grid is the only gradient needed to perform almost all the functions), in a symbolic, stylistic and social universe that would change centuries of urban imagery at its root.

Unlike Scully, I believe that the most important book on architecture of the century that has just come to an end, after *Vers une architecture*, was not *Complexity and Contradiction in Architecture*, but *Learning from Las Vegas*. As early as 1972, and above and beyond its apparent iconoclasm, this had indicated new modes of interpretation and use of the contemporary city, prefiguring an urban form in which signs and figures would have a greater iconological weight than layouts and volumes, breaking down the virtuous genetic duality of the rule that opposed the solid to the void, the landmark to the fabric.
Form is no longer function.

Un-volumetric Architecture

Attempting a brief historical overview, it can be said that Un-vol was born, as a systematic approach, in the 19th century in the paradoxical and magnificent era of enormous and permanent territorial changes on the one hand, and of the ephemeral transformed, through the spectacle provided by the universal exhibitions, into a mass phenomenon on the other.

In fact, while Stonehenge, many of the urban porticoes of the Greeks and Romans, some of the "barchesse" of Palladio's villas, Bernini's colonnades for St. Peter's and Jai Singh's astronomical observatories in Jaipur and Delhi are technically Un- vol, it seems difficult, given the dependence of these parts on the main architectural element or functions connected with the whole, to assign to these works of architecture that degree of functional "superfluity", that propensity for hybridization and multiple use and that capacity to generate space autonomously which are typical of Un- vol.

And while the manifestations of temporal and divine power in the late Renaissance and baroque era (the "machines" for urban triumphs, the parades, the processions, the burnings at the stake of the Inquisition) were popular events that created a temporary mass spatiality, they contained an intrinsic and constant *memento* that the transformation of pomp, discipline or punishment into spectacle was unable to dilute.

In the 19th century, however, two new, contrasting and symmetrical needs stole the scene. On one hand technology demanded to be released from the merely functional specialization of engineering, laying claim to an autonomous aesthetics and imagery on whatever scale they were applied (from the emerging one of street furniture to the great works of infrastructure). On the other, in the age that saw the birth of the first metropolises, the romantic need for a greater interrelation of the individual with the natural environment led to the design of a simulated nature, which required the construction of accompanying artifices (belvederes, gazebos, balconies, mock ruins, footbridges, paths provided with facilities, etc.): devices for establishing not just a visual but also an aesthetic, metaphorical and emotional connection with the landscape. Ever larger swathes of the urban and suburban territory were caught up in this process, turned into parks that functioned as horizontal "sacred mountains" at the service first of the individual and then of the community.

Out of this apparent dichotomy came the Un-vol celibate machine *par excellence*: the Eiffel Tower, a perfect mechanism without any specific function, but which plays the triple role of territorial and mnemonic landmark, monument to technology and privileged means of observing the landscape from an urban plain, giving the crowd for the first time (and it is an emotion that should not be undervalued) the impression of flying.

And, as we have learned from Le Corbusier, the view from above reshuffles the cards of perception. And of planning.

From the communal space to the open space

In the hundred and sixteen years that have passed since the erection of the architectural symbol of Paris, many, too many things have changed in apparently irreversible fashion.

The attention of the discipline has moved away from the urban form, increasingly dominated by vertical layers, by sequences of billboards and decorated sheds that determine the way entire swathes of territory are perceived, and has shifted from the architectural elements to the route and the relations between them (with the road seen as a metaphor of understanding, and therefore of complexity and the opportunity to choose), conceptually transforming static/processional space into the dynamic space of narration, in which the void takes pre-eminence over the solid.

Even the dialogue between figure and ground has once again inverted the relationship between nature and architecture. Paradigmatic of this is the attitude adopted by painting to the problem.

If in the 15th-century *View of an Ideal City* in the Galleria Nazionale of Urbino there is no doubt that artifice takes precedence over nature, the opposite is true of Friedrich's *Ruins of Eldena*, where a fragment of Gothic architecture serves to underline the absolute physical and above all temporal predominance of the natural over the man-made.

But in the pictures of first Hopper and then Hockney (and I am speaking of his paintings with a non-urban setting), the construction and the equipment around it provide a frame of reference for measuring the extent of the change introduced by the modern and then the contemporary attitude: Hopper with his fragments of urban amenities represented in front of scraps of wilderness; Hockney with his paintings of Californian houses that include the swimming pool and landscape. Houses that would later disappear in his extraordinary *Paper Pools*, only to be evoked with precision through the other two elements.

Even apparently certain and unequivocal concepts have in fact changed their role and significance in a very short space of time.

The aesthetic, geographical and semantic character of public space, for example, has been modified.

The coupling of interior with private space and exterior with public space no longer seems valid in the contemporary world: huge multifunctional containers contrast with shelters designed to provide solitude in the open air.

In addition, thanks to the new polycentric forms of settlement that have developed as a result of the increase in mobility and the watering down of the metaphorical value of the city, the road system itself has become a fundamental element of public space, joining the traditional urban voids of the square and the street.

Traditional public spaces, which look more and more often like transient elements of the urban form, cluttered with necessities, services and other facilities that render them increasingly devoid of communal significance and interest, are being replaced by the places occupied by infrastructures, networks and edges, capable of expressing new centralities and new meanings.

Given the semantic and functional inadequacy of public spaces in responding to the ever more urgent need to provide different spaces for a changing society, the objective is no longer just to construct a meaningful urban form, but to investigate the relations between mobility, communal spaces and private spaces.

It is also necessary to point out that networks (of infrastructure, services) and "protected corridors" (of the cultural heritage, ecology, etc.) can be powerful means of reconsidering territory, and that infrastructure represents the skeleton of any form of settlement, even urban sprawl.

So there has been a shift from communal public space to open space.

Until not so long ago a mere consolatory, vernacular and untouchable background, as it was not attractive from the economic viewpoint, the landscape is now regarded as a collective work of art. Patrimony and mainspring of public and private interests that derive benefit from it and guide choices and shifts in production and aesthetics, the contemporary landscape enjoys a complexity of semantic, technical and material differences that is in no way inferior to the multiplicity of urban experiments.

As Lynch reminds us, in his now time-honoured *Wasting Away*, written in 1984 and published in 1990, landscapes (no longer in the singular...) move from one function to another not only because of primary necessities, such as farming, the opening of a major route of communication or the exploitation of natural resources (like dams or mines), but can also radically change their appearance simply to design a new panorama, perhaps more engaging and fascinating than the previous one, or to accommodate, as in the case of ski runs, facilities for recreation and leisure. He goes on to conclude: "the landscape changes by accumulating residues of history".

This reflects a propensity to regard the landscape as a sequence of "spaces in waiting", at different paces of development and with the possibility of more or less lasting interventions.

From the urban ephemeral to the territorial ephemeral, in a "landscape of the provisional" that still has to be investigated and defined, as architecture of complex relations and no longer just of the relations between volumes.

Regressive refoundings

Yet in the post-modern era, idyllic and consolatory backdrops often act as reassuring choruses of accompaniment to refoundings of a regressive type. Faced with the continual rise today in the demand for major works of infrastructure, spaces for free time and large areas for the concentration of consumption and commerce (spaces almost permanently in conflict with the needs of the environment), an aesthetics is gaining ground that rejects the image of flow and complexity, an aesthetics of self-limiting common sense by which only what cannot be seen is acceptable.

Nor do things seem to be going any better for the image of the city: the constant obsession with the concealment of metropolitan reality leads to a dissimulation of the many cities that are now present within the same urban structure behind nostalgic unitary configurations which have now been lost.

The denial of the recent past seems to be the sole condition that the contemporary world is capable of proposing to exonerate itself from its mistakes.

Misunderstandings of the development of today's metropolis lead to a contemporary reinterpretation of the historical city that almost always brings out nothing but its frozen scenery and not the structures of its transformation.

And again: it is believed that the idea of European urban scenery ended with the Second World War, and therefore that no idea of the design of contemporary urban scenery exists or is practiced.

This mistake should be set straight at once: there exists – and how! – a scenery design of the contemporary city (that of commerce, tourism, leisure, just to mention its most obvious aspects), powerful in its economic systems, pervasive in its aesthetic manifestations and well-organized in its political and social modalities. The only difference with respect to the previous one is that it is carried out in fragments that are joined together *a posteriori*, instead of proposing an overall design *ex ante*.

The real problem is that architectural hermeneutics is no longer asked to be the main interpreter of this new design, nor is the architect expected to be an active protagonist, but only a passive spectator. Architecture, in this iconographic and social structure, is often seen as a running dog of the market.

What we might call the interrupted dimension of social space, the politics of fear in the West, deserves a chapter of its own.

Security and its trappings have become the parasitical Un- vol phenomenon *par excellence* of the architecture of volume and communal places. The metal detector is now a planetwide threshold and barbed wire is used as portable fencing. Maintenance and vandalism have become inescapable themes in the planning of new public areas, in a constant involutionary fragmentation of the intimate distance between individuals and the space that surrounds them, to the point of transforming the new sociality into an algebraic product of the intertwining of individual cocoons.

19

Perhaps, as films and books have been telling us for some time, the planning of an open city, constructed without barriers, belongs definitively to our recent past.

So are we heading towards the homogeneity of the European city, where identical functions are housed in similar spaces and where the only difference will be in the relationship between the parts?

The "new city" will probably be slow to reveal itself simply because it is continually changing.

There are also a few questions that remain unsettled.

If in the modern era the narrative structure of architecture and the city was provided by the theme of housing, is there a theme capable of taking its place today, and if so, what is it?

And is looking at the contemporary city as a place of permanent celebration really a necessary way of bringing out the landscape of complexity, or does it serve instead to make clear the landscape of confusion?

And is the landscape, the dominant theme in disciplinary research and experimentation today, really capable of responding with the necessary precision to the demands coming from a society that does not seem to speak in one, collective voice? Or is it about to become a generic field of application for a multitude of lines of research, disconnected from one another in their methods and aims?

What are the strategies for tackling the dichotomies proposed by apparently incomparable scales of intervention? What means can be used to fluidize the relations, not yet resolved, between city, territory and environment, each the vehicle of specific demands that conflict with those of the others? What is the decoder that will allow us to comprehend, even sector by sector, the complexity that surrounds us?

The responses of architecture

The projects that have been assembled in this book make no pretence to forming a unity that will provide a reliable frame of reference and incontrovertible evidence, but focus the gaze on a cheerful modernism, within which more and more space is being given to a joyful, anti-theoretical and anti-rhetorical professionalism: a "fertile eclecticism" (but there are some who claim that eclecticism was the true architectural style of the 20th century in Europe...) that proposes in its entirety an "empirical theory", a new way of looking at the surroundings.

With overall strategies in crisis, along with hierarchies and classifications, and in the ever more urgent need for an updating of terminology and of the approach to design, these works of architecture are no longer subdivided by typological/stylistic families but by categories of urban/territorial use or social modalities, i.e. the way in which their spaces are utilized.

To this freedom in classification corresponds the conviction that Unvol is in fact a heterogeneous theme which brings together different disciplines and anthropic conditions and conceptual scales intermediate between (or different from) the City Plan and the architectural object. That can be the location for reuse of the detritus of contemporary society, for reappropriation, for (re)composition, a place where it will be possible to find a new combination for the elements in play. That uses irony as one of the possible means of adding meaning to the world.

Although technically works of Un- vol do not have an internal space, they do succeed, through a negotiation between environment and landscape, in configuring the open space, a field of operation with qualities and connotations of its own, above and beyond problems of scale, representing in this sense a working counterpart to the criticism of Zevi.

The projects often meet complex challenges, such as defining form without volumetric works of architecture enclosing the space, the articulated coherence of scalar relations with the surroundings, the clarity of structural elements, the epiphany of the discovery of a possible refuge in an architecture which is in appearance wholly extroverted.

Not having to bow to dimensional, regulatory or functional obligations in the strict sense, but almost exclusively constrained by problems of budget, they arrive at a degree of experimentation and stylistic freedom that it would be hard to attain in any other way (and the examples presented here constitute a genuine stratigraphic diagram of contemporary stylistic trends and languages, and all without buildings...). They prefigure lines of technical and linguistic research which, like utopia, tend to be diachronic, aiming to shape the end result directly without passing through the "narrow gates" of the verification and the negotiations of the ordinary and everyday. They can be, in this sense, an act of liberation that counters the so-called "terrorism of history" by sidestepping it, with respect to complex themes such as service structures for archaeological areas, facilities for nature reserves or the landscaping of buffer zones.

In addition, the spatial articulation of the projects defines a frame of operation that, apart from a few glaring exceptions, indicates common instruments, methodologies and objectives.

The first is that of characterizing the spaces (or functions) in which they are located, independently of whether these are situated in the city or outside it, thoroughly investigating the real possibilities of interference and cohesion between sectors of the discipline that are contiguous but now separate (technique, street furniture, restoration, environment, landscape etc.), and almost always trying to be systemic, rather than to produce objects of mere design.

The second is the attitude toward the surroundings: different from the context, but never indifferent to it, in the era of the crowd they try to work by intensity rather than by density, by continuity rather than by permanence (and from this perspective it is easy to understand the extraordinary success of the forms, symbols and thinking coming from the East, cultural matrix of the rarefied and abstract), with objects similar to atmospheric fragments capable, like Oteiza's sculptures, of outlining an idea of interior while remaining exteriors, marking out metaphorical thresholds whose value lies wholly in the relationships with the surroundings.

The third point in common concerns the attitude of the projects towards their potential uses.

While touching almost all the possible uses of open spaces (from rock concerts to places of worship, from interchanges to technological struc-

Jorge De Oteiza
Homage to Mallarmé, 1958

tures, from sports facilities to leisure facilities) and rendering almost tangible the physical dimension of our prosperity defined by urban and territorial architectural systems, the responses that Un- vol gives to the modes of use of its objects are never univocal or prescriptive. The variable structure of Un- vol, the metamorphic identity obtained through its hybrid configurations (collapsible, semi-closed, semi-open, mobile, repeatable, self-built, temporary, etc), the evident diligence of its thinking about construction (in which the vernacular is often regarded as primeval "authenticity", and thus as arcadia) and the constant attempt to recover the sensorial character of architecture and space always seem to stimulate and recount, suggest uses and solutions. Hardly ever do they impose modes of behaviour, evoking instead a playful everydayness that proposes to act as a cultural mediator between an erudite and a popular architecture.

The fact that it is almost a ready-made, an apparently "instant" project that is ready for use, and its constant propensity for multiple modes of use within the same space, for breaking down the boundary between architecture and art, make it the potential motor of a new "diffuse quality", of the kind once advocated in vain by Quaroni.

Just as Land Art has tried to give a figurative character to the "new landscape" of mass society, Un- vol attempts to give it to the "new space" of *surmodernité*. Through "magic" and transcalar objects that help to shape our understanding of the city and the landscape (the oneiric and symbolic value of zero volume should not be undervalued), the architecture reacts to the isotropic grid of the contemporary territory by behaving as what Winnicott calls a "transitional phenomenon" (i.e. one that belongs to the world of illusion but that is at the same time at the base of the beginning of experience): an object of affection able to give a sense of identity and security to the people who pass through those places every day, becoming more important for its significance than for its merely functional use.

Having given up looking for the redeeming project, capable of curing the ills of the community by its presence alone, it seems that architects today have to be as precise as surgeons and as cunning as the Viet Cong, solving problems as best they can and knowing that they each time need to use the wiles of reason and desire to bring architecture back to what is its underlying ethical role: providing a social service.

And no longer a destiny, at last.

"It is a very human characteristic to grope about in the present while musing about the future without realizing that it has already started and is coming round to dinner." (Luigi Pintor)

Burle Marx, *Promenade
of Copacabana,*
Rio de Janeiro, 1970

Surfaces

In its most radical sense non-volumetric architecture is equivalent to the surface. Taking Kandinskij as our starting point, we can consider the point and line as elements very distant from architecture, whereas the surface is now something wholly architectural, sometimes a substitute for the volume itself. This is the case with Burle Marx's promenade at Copacabana. Here Le Corbusier's idea of a sign unifying the city is reduced to a decorated surface that, in a less aggressive manner than a continuous expanse of buildings, creates a horizontal landmark characterizing the city.

Burle Marx's promenade can be considered the moment at which the modern reconciled itself with the surface, freeing itself at last from the shackles of the ideology of early modernity, which distrusted the surface because it was the crime scene of decoration.

In point of fact one of the first to repudiate this ideology was the master of smooth and white surfaces: as far back as the early 1940s, Le Corbusier began to paint pictures on unplastered concrete surfaces. A few years later, at the height of the International Style, the surface freed itself from pictorial influences as well, acquiring substance, texture and thickness. This was the time of repeated ornamental patterns, so-called motifs although they remained confined to vertical surfaces. Post-modernity on the other hand was characterized by a fatal attraction to the surface, discovering that modern language and decoration were not incompatible terms.

At present two interpretations predominate: on the one hand the playful and colourful one of Pop, on the other the rarefied memories of the Zen garden, with its sacred and combed surfaces. The most recent tendencies are attempting to find a common ground between the two interpretations.

Expo '02, Swiss National Expo

1992-2002
Yverdon-Les-Bains,
Switzerland

The "Arteplage" at Yverdon-les-Bains was one of the four sites on which the Swiss National Exhibition was held in 2002. West 8's project was judged the winner of an international competition for the transformation of a riding ground into a landscape with a powerful visual impact. Six-meter-high artificial dunes are the organizing elements of the project: different plants are grown on each dune. Thus visitors wander around a totally artificial landscape, with an ephemeral and psychedelic atmosphere. The park's services are housed in rough wooden structures that blend into the dunes; the sheds are roofed with semitransparent slabs printed with a pattern of flowers.

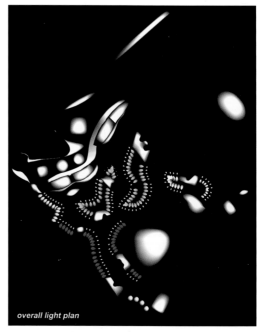

overall light plan

paving: floor treatment and materials

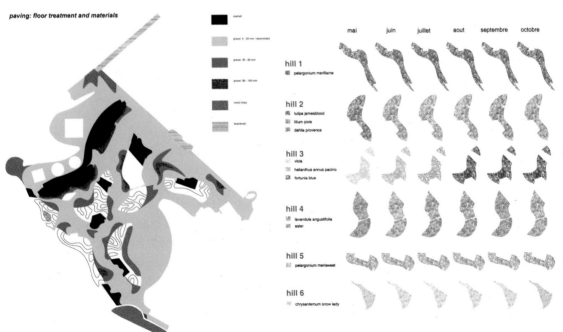

asphalt

gravel: 4 - 20 mm / steamrolled

gravel: 20 - 80 mm

gravel: 80 - 150 mm

wood chips

boardwalk

	mai	juin	juillet	aout	septembre	octobre

hill 1
pelargonium meriflame

hill 2
tulipa jamesblood
lilium pixie
dahlia provence

hill 3
viola
helianthus annus pacino
fortunia blue

hill 4
lavandula angustifolia
aster

hill 5
pelargonium merisweet

hill 6
chrysantemum snow lady

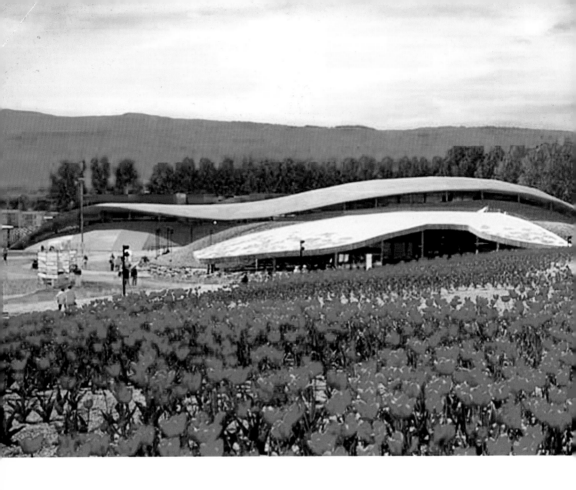

Eduardo Souto
de Moura

Reconversão Da Faixa Marginal De Matosinhos/Sul

1995-2002
Matosinhos, Portugal

The project of reconversion at Matosinhos covers an area of 32,800 m2 and sets out to completely reconfigure the town's seafront by means of a large paved promenade covering a linear underground car park, created to serve both the front of the town and the beach. The characteristic element of the project is a promenade paved with granite flags. It is 19 meters wide and all of 740 meters long and joins such amenities as a bar-restaurant, a sailing school, a discotheque, a swimming pool and the entrances to the underground car park. At Matosinhos the minimal character of the intervention can be seen as a reflection of the desire to create a promenade that would offer an abstract interpretation of the interface between the beach and the town.

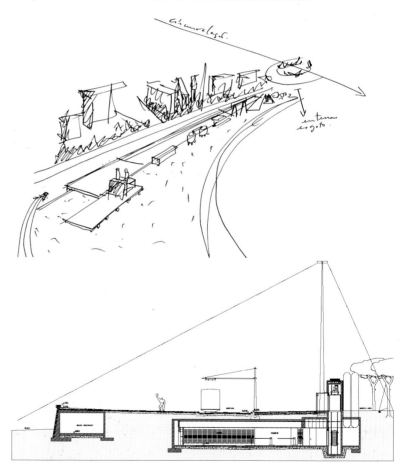

Bernardo Secchi
Paola Viganò

Cemetery of Kortrijk

1994-1999
Kortrijk, Belgium

The project for the new cemetery is situated on a piece of sloping ground at the end of the main road running through the town from north to south, and is set in the rolling landscape of Flanders, emphasizing the slight differences in level. An incision in the ground separates the cemetery from the park. At the entrance a reinforced-concrete wall runs along the edge of an area covered with grass and stone that slopes down to the Hall of Ceremonies. The glass and grating front of the Hall of Ceremonies, whose roof barely emerges from the ground, faces the valley. A long path of packed earth runs down the slope through eleven grass-covered terraces on which the graves will be laid out.

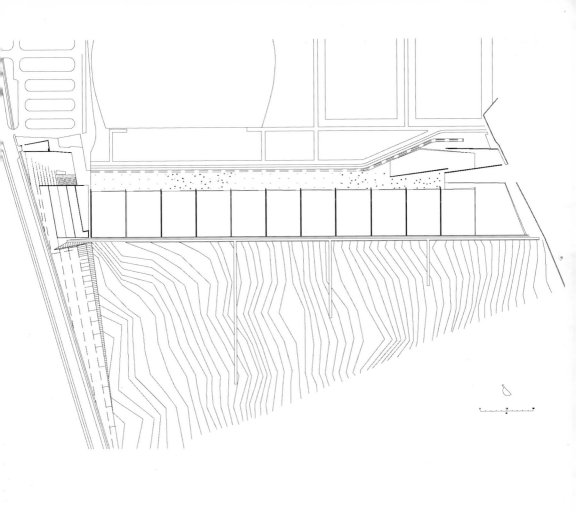

60 Bridges

Liedschreevnen,
Netherlands

The 60 Bridges project was drawn up for a competition held for the construction
of a total of sixty crossings in a new town in the Netherlands. The bridges
are located at the intersection between the urban fabric and farmland. The idea
of the planners was to create a continuous landscape, halfway between the
natural and the artificial. Thus nature "inhabits" the bridge and trees are planted
in the furrows of the prestressed V-beams that support the bridge itself.

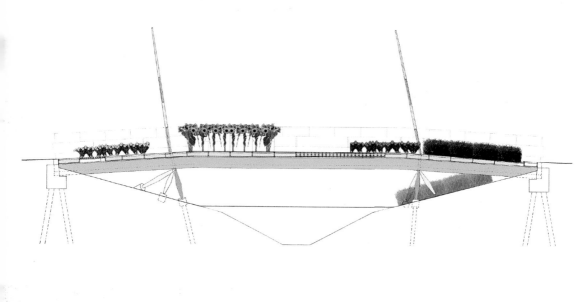

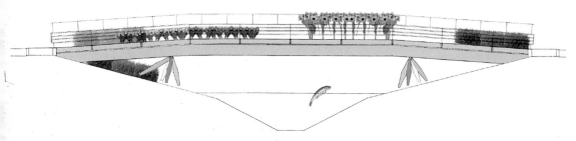

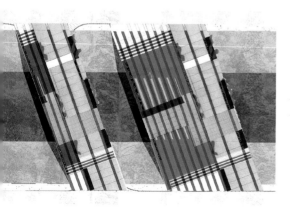

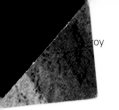

Wolfe Tone Park

Dublin, Ireland

In the project for Wolfe Tone Park we find the same idea of a surface made up of a succession of bands. The six twelve-meter-wide bands of the project organize the paved areas, the plantations of trees, the flowers and the lighting systems, keeping them distinct from one another.

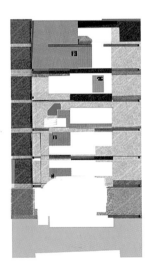

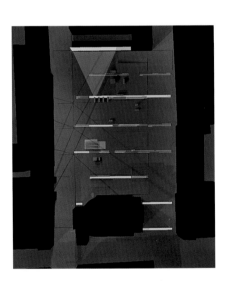

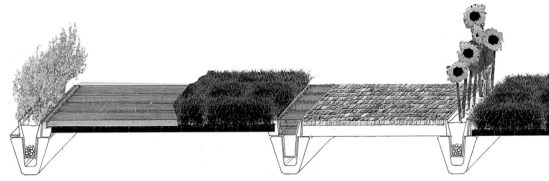

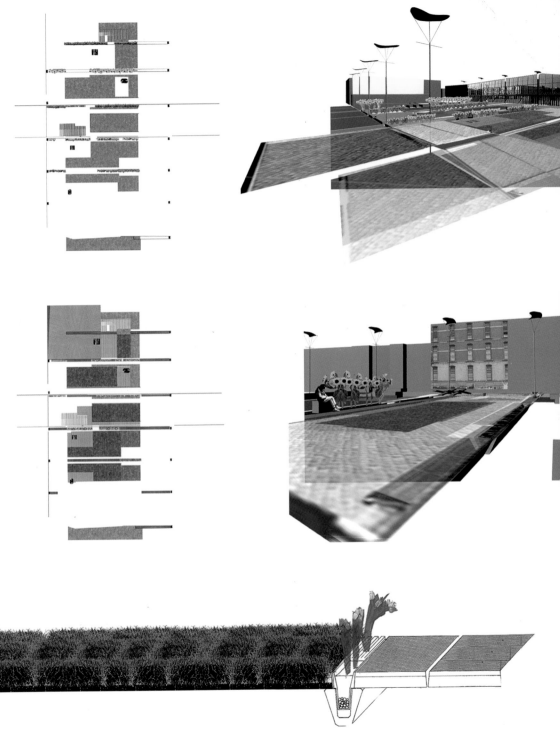

Hideki Yoshimatsu +
Archipro Architects

Cemetery for the Unknown

1997-1998
Mirasaka, Hiroshima,
Japan

Commissioned by the town of Mirasaka, the project is a public memorial and consists of a forest of 1500 two-meter-high steel bars and a succession of earthen surfaces treated in a way that makes them a direct allusion to the Zen garden. The general ambience is in fact that of the Zen garden, where a sense of the sacred is evoked through what is seen, in a mysterious, ephemeral atmosphere halfway between art, nature and architecture.

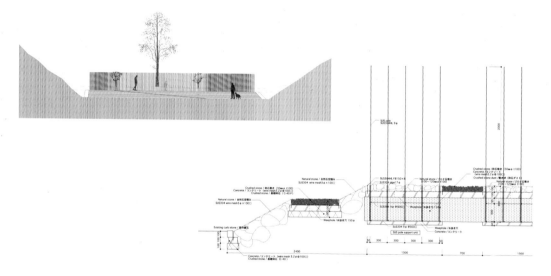

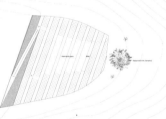

UNIVERSITY
OF SHEFFIELD

EMBT
Enric Miralles
Benedetta Tagliabue

Restauracion del mercado de Santa Caterina

1997-2004
Barcelona, Spain

The research conducted by the EMBT studio has always focused on surfaces, treating them as a support for the genuine decorative accounts that enrich its projects. In the rehabilitation of Santa Caterina Market in Barcelona the upper surface of the roof becomes a suspended plane of narrative, something resembling a magic flying carpet that can be used by the occupants of adjacent buildings. The surface, in honour of Gaudí's Parque Güell, is covered with coloured majolica.

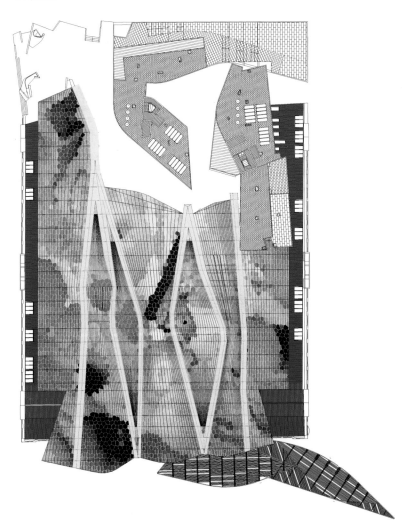

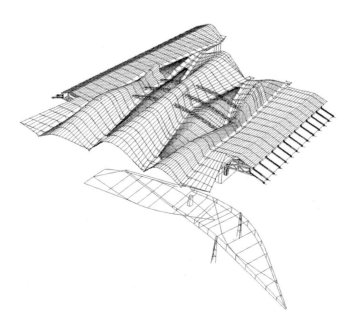

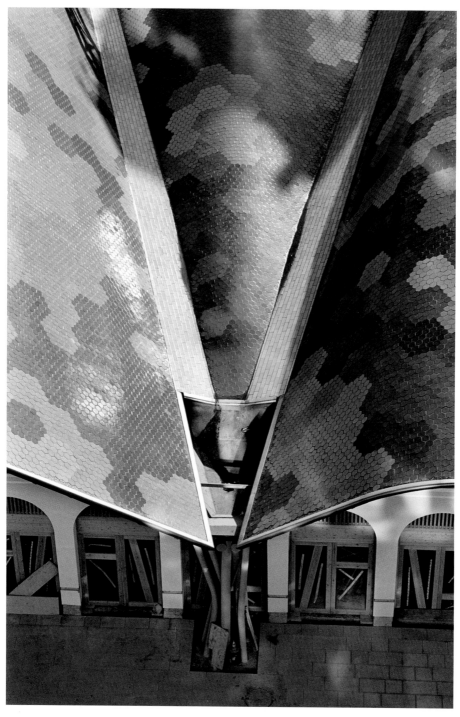

EMBT
Enric Miralles
Benedetta Tagliabue

Parc dels colors de Mollet del Vallés

1992-1995
Barcelona, Spain

The Parco Mollet del Vallés is structured into a narrative sequence of vertical surfaces positioned as elevated screens. They are constructed out of bricks and concrete slabs; the overall impression is something that combines the spontaneous languages of vernacular building with surrealism.

J. Miguel Hernández
León

Murallas de Ceuta

1992-1999
Ceuta, spanish
enclave in Marocco

The plan for the reclamation of the military bastions of the city of Ceuta, built between the 16th and the 18th century by the Portuguese and Spanish, sets out to exploit their potential through a linear and all-embracing design. The intervention consists of the organization of a few materials and plastic elements. The result is a minimal project that works by analogy, where the slanting surfaces of the pre-existing walls are echoed in the slippages in the plan of the new paved areas and where abstraction encounters the Afro-Mediterranean character of the place.

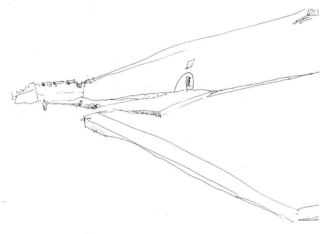

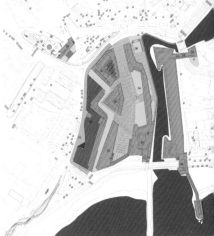

Ira Koers
Jurjen Zeinstra
Mikel van Gelderen

Slijtplein

1997-1999
Amsterdam,
Netherlands

The Slijtplein project covers an area of 3700 m² and is based on the idea of intervening in a nondescript and frayed part of the town through the simple utilization of a piece of ground surfaced with a humble material, asphalt, which has been decorated for the occasion with the outlines of basketball and tennis courts and football pitches. The project is inscribed in the line of the decorated surfaces, adding to this a clear and accessible public function, obtained with the minimum possible means. On top of this it's inserted a certain Pop irony that once again draws on the work of Venturi and Scott Brown and the Site in particular.

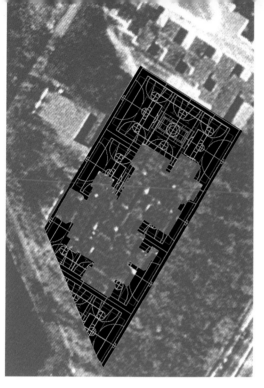

Marcelo Spina
Patterns

Land Tiles, contoured Urban Surface

2003
temporary
installation
Los Angeles, California,
Usa

The Land Tiles are conceived as a means of consolidating the ground and preventing erosion. The principle is that of the repeated pattern and the hypothesis is that of providing instruments of technical design which can transcend mere functionality. The temporary installation is set on the ground and is made up of 140 concrete elements designed on the digital principle of continual uniform variation. The tiles include a continuous flow of water that enhances their appearance and irrigates interstitial patches of grass.

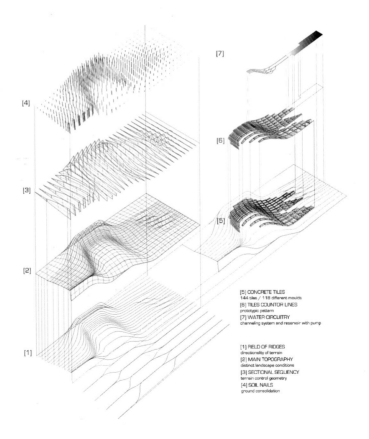

[7]

[4]

[6]

[3]

[5]

[2]

[5] CONCRETE TILES
144 tiles / 118 different moulds
[6] TILES COUNTOR LINES
prototypic pattern
[7] WATER CIRCUITRY
channeling system and reservoir with pump

[1] FIELD OF RIDGES
directionality of terrain
[2] MAIN TOPOGRAPHY
distinct landscape conditions
[3] SECTIONAL SEQUENCY
terrain control geometry
[4] SOIL NAILS
ground consolidation

[1]

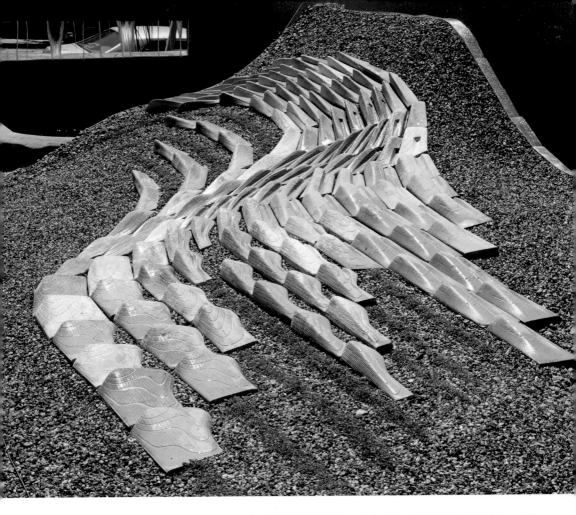

Architecture & Volume (working on the intermediate scale)
Enrico Morteo

Published twenty years apart, two books seem to have exercised a special fascination over the whole of Italian architectural criticism in recent decades. Authentic and irresistible sirens, the two works have given rise to what amounts to a phenomenon of collective hypnosis, and one to which no-one can claim to have been completely immune. Although very different from one another, the books have in common the fact of coming from spheres outside the specific ones of the discipline.

The first of these two books is a literary fantasy, an example of Italo Calvino's cultured and subtle mastery of the genre: the celebrated *Le città invisibili* (1972, *Invisible Cities*). Without presenting a superfluous summary of the book, I will just refer here to the recurrent narrative structure that, as everyone surely knows, turns on the description of a series of fantastic cities, each defined by a distinctive trait so marked and peculiar that it coincides with the identity of the place itself. Instead of looking at the city in all of its modern complexity, produced by the collision of actions, relations, activities, times and energies, Calvino focuses in each episode on a regulating, pervasive and dominant element. Thus Zirma is the city that rouses memories; Isaura, the city of the thousand wells; Zenobia, the city that stands on piles; Eufemia, the city of trade and meetings; Ipazia, the city of things that don't match; Armilla the city built only of water pipes. And so on. The places described by Calvino are marvellous, in the oldest and fabulous meaning of the word, cities saturated with a unique and inimitable significance. As in the stories of the past, in which every city appeared different, inhabited by its own 'spirit' and 'culture'. Betrayed by the failures of urban functionalism, by the inevitable standardization of multiplicity when subjected to cold rational analysis, many architects have found the comfort they had long sought in Calvino's words. Like a leaven, Calvino's cities are insinuated into urban visions, evoked in support of unlikely distortions of the compositional grammar of planning or as specious justifications for pseudo-historicist topographies. In the end all they do is generate a certain amount of confusion between urban morphology and fantasy.

What seems to have escaped many is the nature of the fantastic, so powerfully conjured up by Calvino: the fantastic dimension hardly ever lies in the things that are looked at but in the eyes of the observer. Trying to superimpose the ideas proposed by the book on the actual planning process can only be an effort as titanic as it is vain, an absurd attempt inevitably doomed to vacillate between the nostalgic and the fake.

The second volume is a short ethnological text entitled *Non-lieux* written by the French ethno-anthropologist Marc Augé in 1992. Translated into Italian the following year, within a few months the book had become a genuine manifesto for all those who no longer believed in the possibility of intervening in the contemporary city with the traditional instruments of design and planning. There is no need here to list all the non-places evoked by Marc Augé, but as well as automobiles and expressways, trains and stations, aeroplanes and airports, they included supermarkets, the hotels of the great international chains, car parks and the refugee camps in which people fleeing war and poverty are locked up. Spaces destined to be passed through rather than inhabited, non-places are in Augé's analysis the opposite of the abode and the residence. They are spaces that do not contain and do not comprehend us, and yet are capable of representing the anonymous and globalized way we live with pitiless lucidity. Contrasting and symmetrical with Calvino's invisible and fantastic cities, Augé's non-place is real disorientation, authentic reification of absence, of the lack of relationship and encounter, where the place no longer coincides with the perception of meaning.

Over the last few years there have been a number of projects ensnared by the savage dimension of these new territories of 'supermodernity', almost always neo-Romantic visions of an adventure that is actually only solitude: elevated to an urban scale, the rarefaction of relationships is nothing but a minimalist blow-up of individual misery. Rarer is the proposal of a concrete reflection, an attempt to give sense back to the vacuum of these spaces of passage. Often instead the choice has been to mask this emptiness behind contrived systems of decoration, constructed by consuming at great speed large quantities of images and imaginations, caught between mannered exoticism and futuristic projection in the manner of the science-fiction strip cartoon.

The opposite polarities comprised in these two books have exercised an irresistible magnetism on the analysis of Italian critics, who have ended up contenting themselves with mere chronicling of the present or yearning for the nostalgic revival of strong structures of meaning and value, but in fact incapable of tackling the ever greater vacuum with which design has to deal.

A vacuum produced to a great extent by the effects of the modern technology of communications, responsible for the migration of many of the functions once performed by the spaces of architecture towards virtual places: we talk at a distance, we work at a distance, we meet at a distance. The prefix 'tele-' (from the Greek word for 'far') seems to be the best representation of the contemporary condition. Radically eroded in the public sphere, the possibility of relationship has taken refuge in the private dimension, turning the home into an individualistic nest used to house the authenticity of emotions.

The current trend in architecture is not an isolated case or a theoretical one-off. In many ways, the difficulties encountered by architectural design today reflect similar questions that have already shaken up the universe of industrial design.

The miniaturization of components and the contemporary technological evolution of materials and machines have progressively freed design of the constraints that had long conditioned the definition of form. Where the design had once been defined by the need to establish a connection between the functional mechanisms of objects and the modes in which we use them, electronics has suddenly stripped the form of any real anchorage. In the same way, composite materials, modern techniques of moulding synthetic materials and the integration between material and the artificial intelligence of printed circuits have opened up infinite formal and functional horizons. Without the traditional conditionings dictated by technology and materials, design has more and more clearly revealed its twofold nature as a method of planning and a linguistic system of communication. It suffices to take a brief look at the transformations undergone by one of the objects most emblematic of modernity: the telephone. Originally relegated to service rooms, the telephone timidly found its way into entrance halls and corridors and was then allowed into the living room, from where it went on to conquer every corner of the house, from the kitchen to the bedroom. Ruler of the office, first as switchboard and then coupled with the fax or computer, the telephone has changed a great deal over time and the form of the receiver has altered in step with this evolution, with models that have become part of the history of design, testifying to the changes in our behaviour and the evolution of technology and of our relationship with it: the early candlestick receivers, made famous by American films in which the actor gripped the handle while shouting into a small funnel-shaped mouthpiece and holding a trumpet-shaped speaker to his ear; the celebrated '300' tabletop telephone designed by Henry Dreyfuss for Bell Laboratories in 1937; the unforgettable Ericofon designed by Gösta Thames for Ericsson in 1953; Nizzoli and Oliveri's Sellidor switchboard for Safnat in 1958; Zanuso and Sapper's Grillo phone for Siemens in 1968; the Panasonic KX series of the mid-eighties, combining telephone, fax and answering machine. The appearance of the first portable telephones undermined the static quality of the traditional models, pushing designers of the object in the direction of a semantic surplus: Sottsass came up with the Enorme telephone (with a name that reflected its size) for Olivetti; Armani designed a model of black and cloying elegance; many others reduced the telephone to a mere gadget, concealing it behind the features of comic-strip characters. Flights into irony, luxury or the superfluous that could not halt the evolution of the technology. Nowadays the telephone lives in our pockets and communicates with the computer without wires. Models come out with the frequency of fashion collections and propose versions that look like toys or professional working instruments. But it is not so much appearance that defines its value, as the functions: a telephone today can store data, process information, send or receive e-mail, take pictures, transmit images and receive videos. Incidentally, it can also make telephone calls.

Alongside decorative interventions on the surfaces of objects, the current strategies of industrial design rely on the exploitation of new technological capacities to develop successive typological hybrids, prefiguring modes of use for the objects that act directly on our habits and our patterns of behaviour. This is true not only of complex objects (as in the typological evolution of automobiles, for instance the cumbersome SUVs born out of the encounter between luxury saloon and off-road vehicle), but also of ordinary, everyday accessories. After seasons of runaway success, the world of fashion is transferring the functions of technologically advanced materials into the design of clothing. A process that is having an influence on the form of the clothes themselves and reducing the distance between formal and casual dress. Until a few seasons ago limited to accessories (shoes, watches, glasses), it is now a real trend that is affecting more conventional and codified garments as well, including jackets, pullovers and shirts.

Something of the kind is happening in architecture too, where, along with the muscular display of surprising technological shells, new functional combinations are being tried out. But the reaction times of architecture are inevitably slower than those of industrial design. In addition, focusing attention on the coverings of buildings would mean leaving the emptiness of places unresolved for a long time to come. The things of which the greatest lack is felt are elements capable of connecting the parts, of constructing an account that meanders between the buildings, of providing landscapes capable of accommodating new identities.

Hence it might be useful to re-examine the dimension of museum, exhibition and stage design, a territory halfway between architecture and industrial design. This kind of design does not signify constructing new volumes, nor even intervening in structures, but introducing a privileged point of view that conditions and orients vision. The design of an exhibition is (or rather should be) a filter that modifies not things but our mechanisms of perception.

When Albini designed the rooms of the Genoese museums of Palazzo Bianco and Palazzo Rosso, he did not limit himself to studying a sequence of objects, but introduced a criterion of display that would give prominence to the works: by resorting, for example, to the principle of 'hanging everything', so that every single object was put on display in isolation. In the rooms of Castelvecchio at Verona, Scarpa worked by distinction, separating the old structures from the new surfaces, framing the works in perspective vistas and studying bases and lighting that would highlight them.

Another example of this kind of design is provided by the dynamic spaces of Mollino: his apartments divided up by movable partitions, made to look bigger by strategically placed mirrors and soundproofed by quilted padding, are stages for the performance of our daily lives. Mollino imagined event-spaces, places in which dream and fantasy could emerge. Emblematic of this is his design for the Lutrario Dance-Hall in Turin, a giddy setting for the chance encounter, adventurous territory of the fleeting conquest. A far cry from the anonymous estrangement of the non-place: in this 'station of desire', like on a real stage set, everything is designed to make everyone an actor, a conscious performer of his own role.

Completely different, but no less stimulating, are the countless exhibition designs of the Castiglioni brothers. Let us take the example of the ones that were devoted first to the radio and then to the television, culminating in an extraordinary sequence of stands for the RAI (Radiotelevisione Italiana). Called on to give physical substance to the impalpable

world of sounds and images, the Castiglioni created a series of evocative situations over the span of twenty-two years (from 1947 to 1969) that revealed both the mechanisms underpinning the technological functions and the collective fascination of the new means of communication. Situations that presented the domestic rituals of listening and watching, as well as visual inventions that broke up the uninterrupted flow of sounds and images into three-dimensional graphic compositions: collages of frames, patterns of light, assemblages of sounds that unfolded to the rhythm of radio frequencies. Aerials that turned into forests, television sets scattered around gardens of electro-magical symbols, tunnels of concentrated vision, psychedelic windmills immersed in the darkness: a strategy of surprise that stimulates the observer's perception, in an overall conception of the display as a cognitive X-ray of our behaviour.

Working between things, altering relationships, obliging our senses to confront space, producing situations that throw the proportions of our body and our proxemics out of kilter, acting on darkness or on light, on colour or on depth to reveal the often involuntary relations that we establish with the phenomena that surround us.

Adopting the approach taken by exhibit and stage design, architecture might be able to intervene more effectively in urban patterns of behaviour, suggesting new interpretations and different modalities in the use of the spaces of the city. A line of attack that may be reminiscent of the procedures of industrial design, but which could above all restore to these places something of the marvellous quality of Calvino's cities.

In Rio de Janeiro, designing the twenty kilometres of sea front that unite the Museum of Modern Art and the beach of Leblon, passing by the beaches of Flamengo, Botafogo, Leme, Copacabana and Ipanema, Roberto Burle Marx not only produced the greatest urban landscape in the world, but was able to create a special place, shaping the transition between the city and the ocean. On one side the houses, offices and transactions of everyday commerce; on the other the boundless and inexhaustible expanse of the sea. In the middle the beach, favourite stage of recreation, temple dedicated to the rites of amusement and care of the body. Burle Marx's promenade reflects an awareness of the fact that the city faces onto a different dimension, of the gap between the time occupied by work and the free time of leisure. A slow lane through the city, the promenade is a belvedere opening onto the teeming expanse of bodies, an intermediate space between the flow of vehicles and the bathing costumes. Here designs traced on the ground accompany the strollers or mark the passage of rollerskaters, bicyclists and skateboarders; they indicate the places where you can stop to drink coconut water or sit and chat. What Burle Marx was able to do was liberate the pavement from the flat two-dimensionality of supergraphics: the ground has gained the fourth dimension, that of time, divided up into moments of pause, acceleration and relaxation. Not even one cubic meter, nor a precious catalogue of public amenities, but elements of a new urban geography for citizens temporarily at their ease. Architecture is not made of volume alone.

Bibliography

W. Benjamin, *Berliner Kindheit um Neunzehnhundert*, Suhrkamp Verlag, Frankfurt 1950.

I. Calvino, *Le città invisibili*, Einaudi, Turin 1972 (Eng. trans. *Invisible Cities*, Picador, London 1979).

M. Augé, *Non-lieux*, Seuil, Paris 1991 (Eng. trans. *Non-Places*, Verso, London-New York 1995).

Rassegna 58 "Dichiarazioni d'interni: appartamenti italiani 1947-1993", ed. by M. De Giorgi and M. Romanelli, Editrice CIPIA, Bologna 1994.

E. Morteo, 'Suolo pubblico', in *Modo*, no. 181, July–August 1997.

S. Polano, *Achille Castiglioni*, Electa, Milan 2001.

D. Scodeller, *Livio and Piero Castiglioni. Il progetto della luce*, Electa, Milan 2003.

M. De Giorgi, *Carlo Mollino. Interni in piano-sequenza*, Editrice Abitare Segesta, Milan 2004.

E. Morteo, *Il futuro del design* (in course of publication), UTET, Turin 2005.

Luis Barragán and Mathias
Goeritz, towers for the
Ciudad Satélite of Mexico
City, 1957

Historically, vertical architecture with no internal space corresponds to the monument. No date can be given for the origin of this configuration: it is an archetype found in all civilizations. From the 19th century onwards the monument transmuted its transcendent symbolism into an increasingly evident physicality, into a collective visual point of reference and finally into toponymy. So it is no accident that in his 1960 essay *The Image of the City*, Kevin Lynch spoke of landmarks, i.e. points of reference that are no longer symbolic but visual, and as such include not just monuments but also advertising hoardings, objects of urban design and even natural elements. In general the modern era, despite having often professed an anti-monumental spirit, has left us vertical presences that have been able to turn abstract language into collective narrative. The prime examples are the Eiffel Tower and its logical evolution, Tatlin's monument to the Third International. After the war the abstract and mechanical interpretation of the vertical monument rediscovered figurative language. At Chandigarh and Brasilia Le Corbusier and Niemeyer took on not just modernity, but also tradition and the landscape, and they did it once again by referring to sculpture. But the dimension was no longer that of the city, but that of the city-territory. The vertical monument then established itself in areas cleared of buildings, in large empty spaces, as in the case of the towers that Louis Barragán constructed with Mathias Goeritz for the Ciudad Satélite of Mexico City.

Since the 1970s non-volumetric architecture of a vertical character has grown less and less sculptural and more and more architectural. This permits these configurations to be turned into collective, liveable and usable events. Although non-volumetric architecture has put its metaphysical image behind it for good, it has not renounced the symbolic aspirations necessary to communication in a mass society.

Venturi,
Scott-Brown
& Associates

Master plan,
Denver Civic Center Cultural Complex

1995
Denver, Colorado, Usa

In the early nineties the Colorado Historical Society, Denver Public Library and
Denver Art Museum, asked the designers to draw up a master plan that would be
able to bind the three institutions together into an urban unit. The plan focused
on an area of five blocks that comprised the three institutions and their car parks.
The project started out from an overall vision of the urban fabric of Denver and
more specifically the Golden Triangle, the district to the south of the Civic Center
Park.

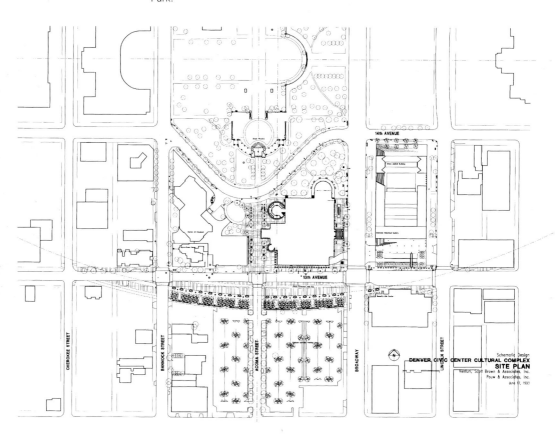

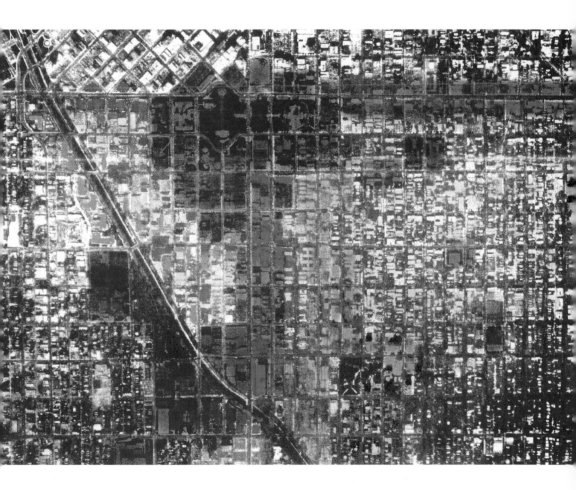

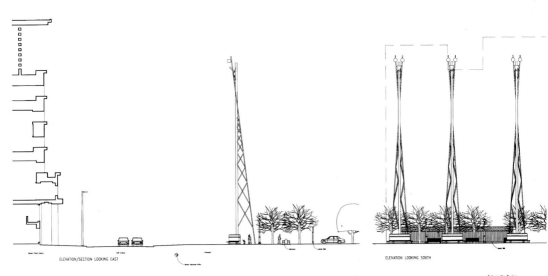

ELEVATION/SECTION LOOKING EAST

ELEVATION LOOKING SOUTH

Schematic Design
DENVER CIVIC CENTER CULTURAL COMPLEX
ARC ELEMENT ELEVATIONS
1" = 8'-0"   Venturi, Scott Brown & Associates, Inc.
Pouw & Associates, Inc.
June 17, 1993

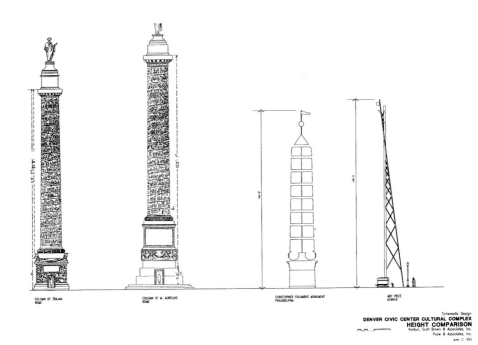

COLUMN OF TRAJAN
ROME

COLUMN OF M. AURELIUS
ROME

CHRISTOPHER COLUMBUS MONUMENT
PHILADELPHIA

ARC PIECE
DENVER

Schematic Design
DENVER CIVIC CENTER CULTURAL COMPLEX
HEIGHT COMPARISON
Venturi, Scott Brown & Associates, Inc.
Pouw & Associates, Inc.
June 17, 1993

67

Toyo Ito   **Tower of winds**

1986
Yokohama - Shi,
Kanagawa, Japan

The Tower of Winds is a 21-metre-high structure with a cylindrical surface
that houses the ventilation ducts and water tanks of a shopping centre located
underneath the tower. The tower is clad with a double membrane of reflective
panels on the inside and perforated aluminium on the outside. By day the tower
has a physical presence and volume, but at night this is dematerialized
in a genuine visual metamorphosis, amplified by a striking use of artificial illumination.
The intensity of the artificial light is adjusted by a computer on the basis of the
number of decibels produced by the traffic and the direction and strength of the
wind. The tower has been demolished at the end of the ninetines.

Coop Himmelb(l)au   **Expo 02 Forum Arteplage Biel**

1999-2002
Arteplage Biel,
Switzerland

The three filigreed towers for Expo 02 at Arteplage Biel stand at the end of a pier extending into the lake. It was the intention of the designers to present something that would be reminiscent of the world of airports. The platform is conceived as a large promenade on which the individual pavilions of the exhibition are set. By day the towers look like a family of giants and at night are transformed into sculptures of light that emphasize the transitory character of the Expo. The platform covers an area of about 16,000 m² and the towers vary in height from 35 to 43 metres and have a steel structure faced with panels with small holes in them.

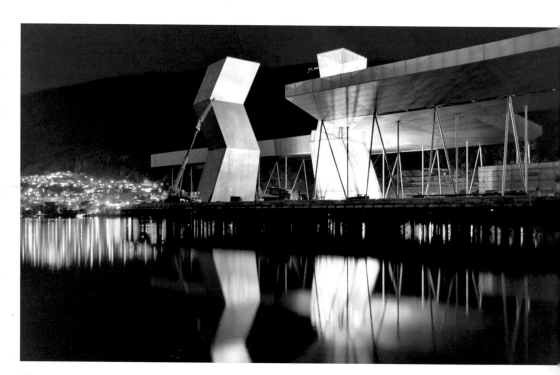

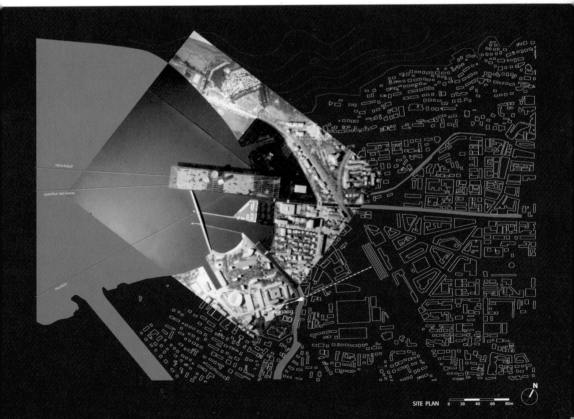

SITE PLAN 0 20 40 60 80m

Richard Horden
T.U. Munich

Wing Tower

1993
Glasgow, UK

The project for the Wing Tower won an international competition for a 140-metre-high tower in Glasgow. The design is intended to satisfy aerodynamic requirements and the tower, which has a steel structure weighing 300 tonnes, rotates to follow the direction of the wind. The movement is controlled by a computerized system linked directly to weather forecasting centres. On top of the tower is set a viewpoint, accessible by lift.

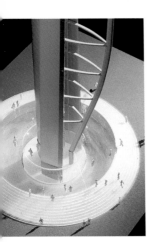  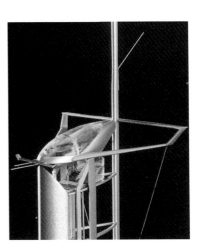

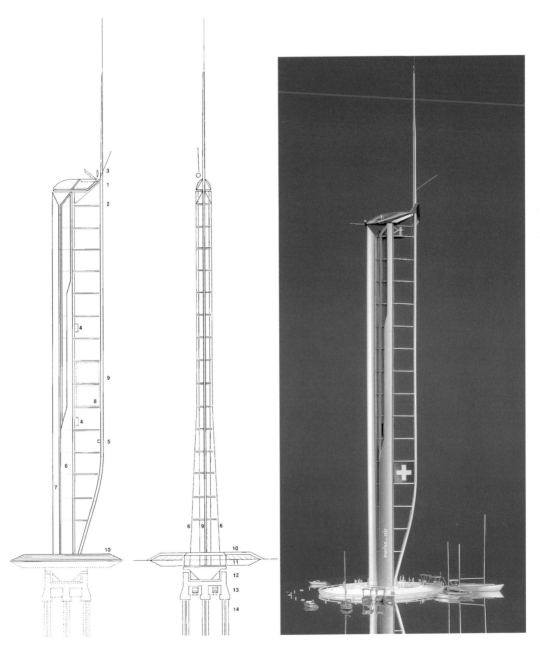

Richard Horden
T.U. Munich

Peak Lab, high altitude Research Station
on the Kleine Matterhorn

2003
Zermatt, Switzerland

The Peak Lab is a project for an observatory set high in the Alps and is conceived with ultralight materials, easily transported by helicopter and assembled on site. The tower is self-sufficient as far as energy requirements is concerned.

transport/construction
10.500,- € / 16.000,- CHF

support system
20.000,- € /30.000,- CHF
1.200 kg

foundation
15.000,- € / 22.600,- CHF

top
8.000,- € / 12.200,- CHF
400 kg

module_1
21.000,- € / 32.000,- CHF
900 kg

module_2
36.000,- € / 54.800,- CHF
1.100 kg

module_3
19.000,- € / 29.000,- CHF
900 kg

module_4
25.000,- € / 38.000,- CHF
1.100 kg

Ville Hara
Helsinki University

Kupla – The Bubble: Korkeasaari Zoo Lookout Tower

1999-2002
Helsinki, Finland

The tower, ten metres high, has been designed with the aid of a series of models that were used to demonstrate the structural behaviour of the curved wooden planks empirically. The last of these models, on a 1:5 scale, was two metres high. The tower was designed and built with the constant assistance of students at the Wood Studio Workshop, who over the space of three months erected this filigreed structure which has become a transparent landmark on the island of Korkeasaari, opposite Helsinki. Notwithstanding the formal complexity of the tower, it is constructed out of planks with a constant section bent into seven different shapes and assembled with simple joints.

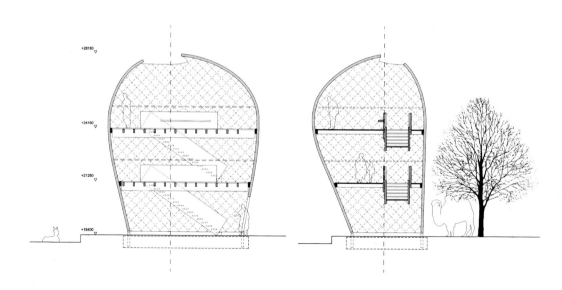

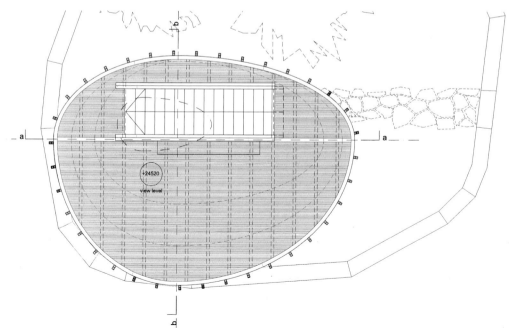

Renzo Piano
Building Workshop

Bigo

1985-1992
Genoa, Italy

The 'Bigo' in Genoa was built as a symbol of the great urban renewal undergone
by the city on the occasion of the five hundredth anniversary of the discovery
of America by Christopher Columbus. The 'Bigo' is a gigantic piece of stage
machinery set down at the centre of the old port. The crown of poles, alluding
symbolically to life in the port, emerges from the sea, and on one side hangs
the roof of the adjacent wharf, while on the other is set a panoramic lift designed
to turn the city into a spectacle for public enjoyment. Given its significance, the
'Bigo' can be considered to all intents and purposes a symbol of non-volumetric
architecture in the age of mass tourism.

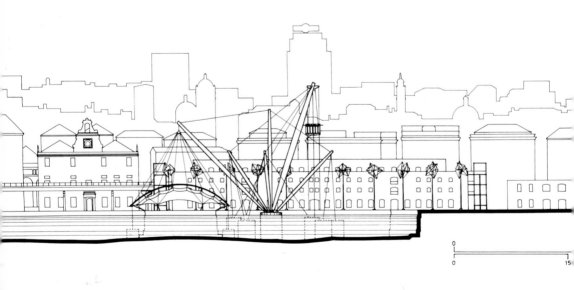

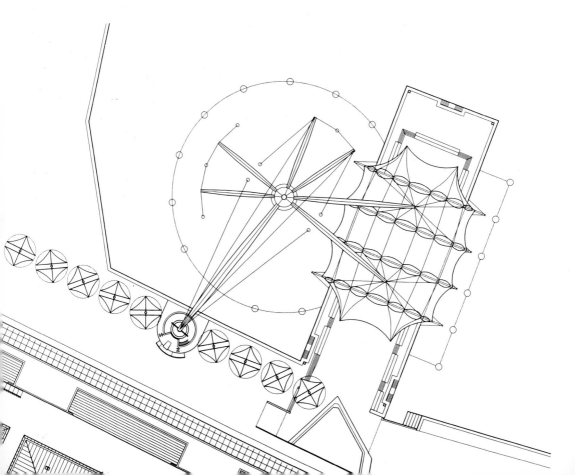

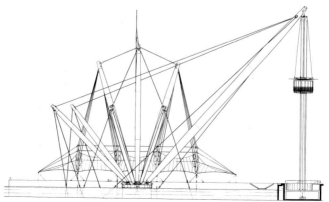

Enric Miralles

Meditation Pavilion

1991-1993
Unazuki, Japan

At the point where the ancient Unazuki trail traverses the deep valley of the Kurobe river there used to stand a footbridge, now transformed into a bridge for heavy traffic. The foundations of the old crossing have been used to build this resting place, conceived as if the path wound around itself, rising in fragments. The steel structure is also designed to house temporary bamboo constructions that celebrate the different seasons.

Tour de Belvedere

2003
Bos Van Ypeij,
Friesland, Netherlands

The Belvedere Tower is made up of an internal walkway that leads to an observation platform on the top and faces on the inside onto an exhibition space underneath the ramp. The tower is 35 metres high and is based on the gradual transformation of the walkway, which has a gentle slope at the bottom but grows steeper as it rises, turning into stairs at certain points. The façade also follows the principle of variation according to height, offering different views of the surrounding area.

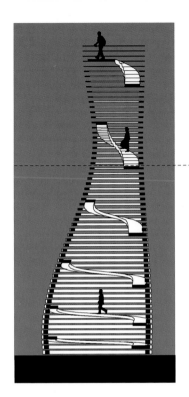
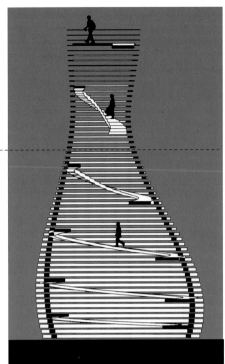

Oswald Zoeggeler

Monument for the E3-E5 Motorway Junction

1972
Bruxelles, Belgium

The monument is located at the point of intersection of two important European motorways, running from Portugal to the countries of the East and from Scotland to Sicily. The large object was intended as a reminder that any possibility of a united Europe depended on communication routes.

A gigantic anemometer underlines the circular movement of the traffic beneath. By means of a dynamo, it produces the electric power that serves to illuminate the monument at night and create a pillar of light that is projected into the sky.

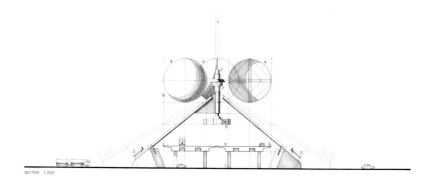

SECTION 1:200

1 LIGHTCOLUMN
2 REFLECTOR
3 GENERATOR
4 PADDLE
5 NATIONAL FLAGS
6 MOTORWAY E3
7 MOTORWAY E5
8 MODULOR - 8 m

PLAN 1:200

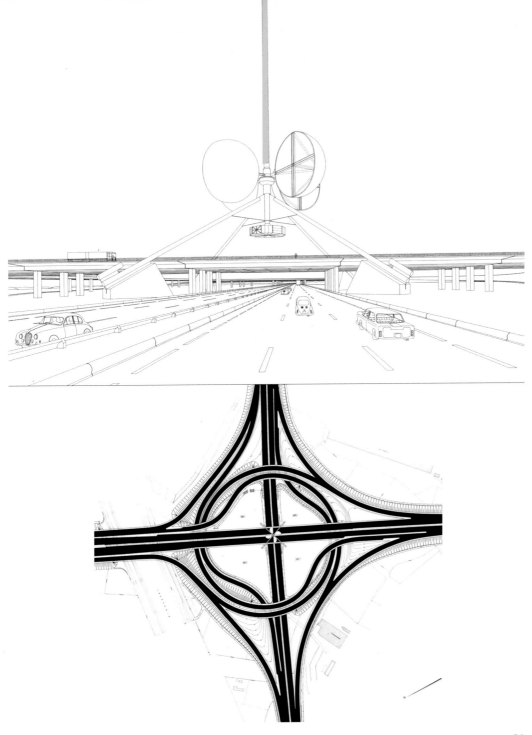

Massimiliano Fuksas   **Musée des Graffitis. Entrée de la Grotte**

1988-1993
Niaux, Ariège, France

The project is conceived to create an assembly and interchange point between the car park underneath and the level of the cave with its famous wall paintings dating from 11,000 BC. The metaphor is that of a large prehistoric animal emerging from the cave and spreading its wings to attract visitors. The wings are made of Cor-ten steel and the walkways on the ground are built of wood.

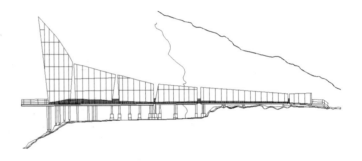

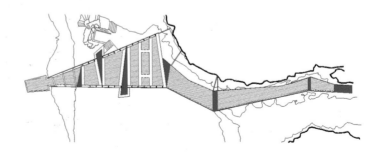

Un-volumetric architecture and the emergence of the architectural
Wes Jones

To understand the proposition that there can be an un-volumetric architecture, it is necessary to believe that architecture may be divided away from a simple limiting congruency with the necessarily spatial, that is, with buildings. This possibility may be noticed today for two reasons: first, because technology has leapfrogged beyond the limits that architecture traditionally helped to establish, and gained a vantage point from which to see those limits as provisional rather than absolute. And second: because a generation of architects has come of age that were raised with this viewpoint, "outside the discipline", in a climate hostile or at least indifferent to the idea of a continuing tradition. Now that technology is capable of producing a virtual reality that deserves the name, and that reality has in turn been granted a value surpassing the "real" by this generation of computer-suckled youth (now that reality has become "so called", in other words), aspects of architecture once assumed to be fundamental, like shelter or volume, or even presence, may not be taken for granted.

The present "liberation" of architecture from old technology is fundamentally different from the evolutionary progress of the past. It has recast that progress as more like stylistic misalignments (between successive technologies and their architectural assimilation) than substantive changes. The history from which the common sense of architecture has been built, and from which it draws its confidence, holds no lessons for the application of a technology that can ignore gravity and presence. The canon will not hold when contemporary practice is torn from an exclusive relation to building by virtual reality, and when it is taken out of the hands of the professional by nanotechnology.

While the answer to what this next wave of technology will liberate architecture from is all around, it is not clear there is any possible answer to the question of what it will be a liberation to. This confusion is more than the reasonable hesitation before an uncertain future. It is a tremor before the possibility of no future. The anachronisms of the nineteenth century's classical Roman ordination of steel or Rome's own earlier trabeation of arcuated concrete were duly corrected once the tectonic character of the new technology was apparent, but in the present case the advances come without the possibility of tectonic guidance. In fact, the current threshold marks the end of such assimilation, as it marks a complete liberation from the physical limitations that the succession of technologies addressed.

The "avant-garde" has reacted to this new technology as if it were a liberation from an overly constraining necessity. Things once considered sacred about architecture are subject to new scrutiny preservation or increase, but with an indifference to their fate. To those who look at it this way architecture must seem like a game with no consequences, from which they themselves might walk away once the play can no longer sustain conviction. The signs of this are everywhere, from the post-critical relinquishment of responsibility to the formalism that takes such relinquishment as a license to be silly, from the obsession with "branding" and consumer culture (in a bid for what passes today for relevance), to the retreat from building altogether in a defensive haze of academic obscurity and formal slackness.

What actually is at stake in this freedom, though? It is not buildings that are threatened by the coming technology, since shelter will always be necessary. Nor is it space, per se, since there will at least always be a human presence to fill it. And not even the profession, since a litigious society will always require licensed responsibility to blame. What is at risk is the glue that binds these together into a discipline, with a coherent sense of the architectural. Not shelter, but the architectural sense that it matters enough to ennoble; not space, but the architectural affect to which it may aspire; not the profession, but the architectural spirit that occasionally makes it a vocation instead of a business.

It is this coherent sense of the architectural that is precisely what is preserved in un-volumetric architecture, and thus what must remain even after everything else is lost. If architecture is traditionally "located" at the convergence of space, building and art, it could be shown that the many faces of architecture through history can be explained in terms of the different proportions of this mix, and it is this proportionate mix, rather than any of its constituents, that carries the gene of the architectural.

When space and a definitive relation to shelter or building are eliminated from an accounting of the necessary in architecture, and with them a sense of public/civic responsibility, what is left? The consideration of architecture from an un-volumetric perspective might be an important first step toward strategizing architecture's survival in a future where these traditional underpinnings are missing or uncertain. Where is the architectural in (the experience of) architecture? This question could, of course, have always been asked, and often was, but always from inside a question worth asking.

If it is not to be found in the object itself or in the space enclosed, as a quality of affect, or in the relation between these, is it then an artifact of the frame that identifies the experience, or is it merely a conventional product of labor, legislated into particularity by licensing and practice? Is architecture an effect of the social or power relations that meet on any site, the history that has been effaced by the newer construction or the potential it suggests? It is architecture's secret that it is conventional, and a relatively simple matter to consider each of these physical construction, the space as enclosed volume, the experience, practice, the social dimension architecture.

The term "the architectural" (rather than simply "architecture") might be advanced to refer positively to a general case of architecture-ness, one not fettered to specific, isolated products that might be prompted by a greater variety of object-stimuli, or variety of stimuli within a single object. Thus, not specific instances of architecture, invariably buildings, but a broad, and exportable, sense of the architectural, that could be applied to or explain a wider range of experience[1].

Indeed, it is possible to see the evolution of architecture's institutional identity from being simply a better thing into a different kind of thing as what has led eventually to its present day marginalization. When Hugo claimed that the printed word would bury architecture he could have been talking about architecture's disciplinary self-imprisonment, as well as its fixity or localization. Having lost a primary connection with stuff, and thereby the ability to stand in judgement as the best stuff, architecture finds that its un-consumable kind is just not that important anymore in a fast-paced consumption-oriented world, and it is not asked to speak for stuff in general.

As a metaphor already in use, architecture evokes useful qualities of fixity, structure, organizational character, stateliness, order. These characteristics of the architectural are exportable because they make sense in translation and can be understood apart from a relation to space or shelter. Architecture's assumed permanence or physicality may lend such borrowings an unintended irony, as when Fashion uses "architecture" to describe a particularly structured design, for example, or computer scientists take it to label the fundamental organization of a virtual system. It is a sign of how commonplace this has already become that this irony is unrecognized, and of how established as well that such irony is denied when pointed out. But, since an assay of the architectural-outside-architecture identifies those aspects not exclusively related to building or space, then their circumstances in new surroundings might be instructive in understanding an architecture less dependent on space or building as well. This external appreciation is an immediate precursor of the more violently shifted perspective the new technology will bring; the reflection of this external appreciation back into the field is already influencing the value system of the field today, and in some quarters superseding it. Old-school critics within the field welcome this as a breaking down of conventional, disciplinary barriers, while old-school practitioners fear it as the same thing; the youngest, accustomed to such openness from Playstation©, may not notice any of this. If it is in fact the architectural behind this, the diffusion of the architectural is shown in a different light, as perhaps a natural release from its imprisonment within space or building. When the security of its traditional prison cell is threatened by advances in technology, this heretofore dormant protean possibility becomes a means of self-preservation[2].

This protean character is architecture's strength, allowing it to stand for permanence despite its own continual redefinition, while it has also allowed it to enrich itself by borrowings, leaving architecture without any incontrovertible core about which to circle its wagons when it is threatened. Indeed, it is what makes the circling of the wagons itself the "architectural", and what makes the architectural slip any implications of space in that circling.

Architecture can be fractionated to the relationship among five characteristics, of which three are necessary and two conventional. The architectural emerges as a residue in this cracking of architecture: what remains when the necessary aspects of architecture are considered separately from the conventional. The five are: intentionality, importance, adherence to limits, relation to space, or volume, and a relation to shelter, or building. The other attributes commonly associated with architecture can be seen as specific cases of these. Order, for example, is really a response to the issue of limits that foregrounds intentionality, while fixity or endurance can be seen as a result of importance. The technological trends referred to above are forcing a reappraisal of this array, with the result that the two that are historically conventional, volume and building, may fade away or simply drop out as irrelevant, leaving a precipitate of intentionality, importance and limits as the architectural. The terms, as well as the qualities they name, have a long history together, and the language itself has evolved during and as part of that history, so that they may not be as cleanly separable as this discussion might suggest. Nevertheless, it is useful to consider them at least for their particular contribution to the whole.

What can be distilled from the traditional relation to buildings and shelter is the quality of intentionality. The conventional support of program or function may be understood in a more refined and exact way as an embrace of the intentionality or purposefulness they codify. Intentionality beyond the necessary, that is beyond shelter, is what conventionally elevates building into architecture. Because of this transcendence of necessity, this intentionality is raised in architecture to a level beyond that of any other built object that gives evidence of intention, while other objects do not wear that fact in the (self-conscious) way that architecture does. The difference between art and architecture, recast along this axis, clarifies architecture's uniqueness. Art is consumed in its intentionality, but with no purpose beyond the signification and celebration of itself, whereas the intentionality of architecture is always transitive: architecture may be art, but it is never just that. Only bad art is programmed or functional in the way that architecture cannot escape. Even as it leaves space or building/shelter behind, "function" will leave a residue that distinguishes architecture from art and from building in the character of its intentionality.

The character of that intentionality also owes something no doubt to the original, Vitruvian sense of importance (beyond simply the intention to build) underlying the well known triad of commoditas, firmitas, venustas. It was this that caused him to single out the arche-tecton's work as architecture. This importance is not necessarily derived from a program but from the attention paid during design. Thus stuff deemed unimportant by virtue of its program or function may be invested with the stateliness or nobility that signals architecture by the expenditure of greater design intention. The judgement of importance is different from that of good design, though, since things deemed important as architecture may in fact be poor designs, while some good designs may not necessarily be understood as architecture. The ability to stand in judgement is dependent on a connection to what is judged, which is possible because of the transitive nature of architecture's intentionality, but it is the judgement that makes it matter.

Importance and intention do not complete the picture, though. Missing is that quality of organization/design that stems from a conscious, willed appreciation of limits. If intentionality gets it going, and its relative importance sustains it, then limits keep it on track. It is the specific limits that make intentions and importance into architectural intentions and architectural importance. These limits are often interpreted as an overt structuring or perhaps a restriction to a class of professional practice. Such limits are easily seen in operation as the historical interest in symmetry, regularity, hierarchical balance, for example, or as a continuing fact of professional licensure. Architecture is a superlative of building because it is limited to certain examples. "Limit" also has another side, though. A more complex understanding of the two sides of the role of the limit was introduced by Deconstruction, which sees architecture on the one hand as "no more than the strategic effect of the suppression of internal contradiction. It is not simply a mechanism that represses certain things. Rather, it is the very mark of repression" (Wigley, The Architecture of Deconstruction, p. 209), and then on the other claims that "The institution of architecture is not concerned the construction of buildings, but with the maintenance of the idea of building" (Wigley 217). Both sides of the limit are represented: the negative side of it as circumscribing possibility, and the positive or "constructive" side of it as providing the possibility (in that circumscription) for meaning or significance. These rehearse the view from the inside and outside as providing identity.

The obverse side of imposed limit-as-constraint is self-imposed restraint. Indeed, architectural design could be considered the alchemical conversion of constraint into restraint. Architecture is not usually thought to be subject to limits in this way: the envelope is generally assumed to be pushed, rarely is it seen positively as an effect of restraint. When the propriety of a particular effort is questioned, such restraint is highlighted, and the conventional nature of the limit is revealed. When a new material like steel suddenly expands the range of physical possibility, form holds back from exploiting this new territory until it can be disciplined. It is only with the hindsight of history that the actual location of the limit comes to be known, since the sense of propriety itself changes with the limits it protects. This puts the design effort at the fuzzy edge where conviction and uncertainty trade influence, where genius is suspect and lunacy given a chance.

On the other hand, as the deconstructivist would point out, the label "architecture" is itself a limit (usually in relation to certain objects it excludes all others). Limits locate the object, within the universe of possibility. Not only as possible, but as particular. This and not that. As de Saussure shows for language, a world is implied by this particularity, suggesting the range of potential relationships it may make with others. In this sense, such limits bring a sort of security with them, and with that a quality of importance. The complex supplemental relationship this describes between the frame and its contents permits architecture's simultaneous openness to change and confidence in continuity that seems to encourage episodic reconsideration of the specifics of its identity: the variety that has found a home inside that frame through time. Such reconsideration does not exclude the possibility that there might be a thread connecting these experiences across time and exigency, though. In anticipation as much of the loss of this thread, as in demonstration of the openness of this frame, architecture is already being bled off into other areas like product design and interface design, unintentionally from within (branding/blobs) and opportunistically from without. It is exquisitely ironic that this recalls the broader sense of architecture that Vitruvius originally described, when the term encompassed many things unrelated to buildings. For him, what fit inside the frame was not just buildings but (as the de-constructeurs repeat) building itself construction.

These limits were established over time as physical boundaries of the possible and this made them seem unchosen and incontrovertible. Which made the important effect of straining against those limits. Yet, at the same time we must stumble when that against which we push is suddenly removed and our brilliant force spends itself on thin air. At that point architecture is revealed to be self-important. The avant-garde is the clearest example of this: celebrated for "pushing the envelope", but never heralded for technical innovation. Its particular form of celebrity shows these limits for what they really are: not a physical constraint, but an achievement of restraint. As the avant garde explores the territory opened up by technology their sensible actions in the unmapped terrain start to lay down the new limits.

None of these characteristics of the architectural entails either space or building necessarily. Of course, they include both as possibilities. In this sense, then, the modifier "un-volumetric" is becoming unnecessary, even as a critical challenge to convention, because the architectural is, already, losing its relationship to volume. But it is useful still if the purpose is to facilitate the liberation of the architectural from architecture.

[1] A generosity to other forms of embodiment is not foreign to the historical idea of architecture. Vitruvius understood architecture as embodying a distinction of degree rather than kind, across a general variety of things: those that are produced by the arche-tecton, or first worker, as opposed to secondary workers, rather than the products of one type of worker or one kind of material. The profession as it is known today is generally considered to have been invented by Brunelleschi, who also painted (inventing perspective), and sculpted (the duomo doors), and worked on buildings as much as an engineer (the duomo dome) as an architect. Even after Alberti narrowed the focus to buildings with his distinction between design and construction, architecture admitted the services of polymaths like Michelangelo and Jefferson.

[2] Within architecture, this attractive exportable aspect is more or less synonymous with its tectonic (attributes). The discourse of tectonics, which emerged at the same time as the discourse about architecture's essential relation to space, is the language for discussing architecture as stuff. And Frampton, at least, sees that as sufficient to a definition. He would not exclude spatial implications from a discussion about tectonics, since he is more concerned with promoting tectonics as a grounding principle that might prevent architectural expression from becoming commodified, but neither does he see space as prior or more essential.

Winsor Mc Cay, *The little Nemo in Slumberland*, 1908. Strip cartoon from the New York Herald, 1908, July 26th

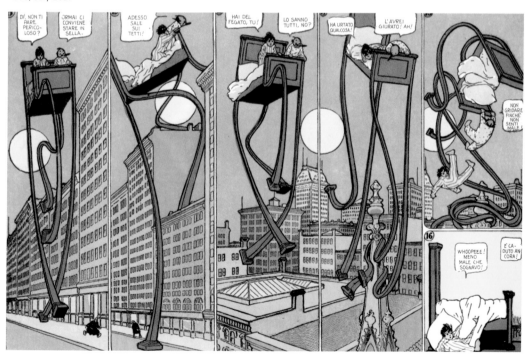

Luciano Baldessari, Breda
Pavilion at the Milan trade
fair, 1952

Enclosures

In antiquity the enclosure was the *temenos*, the sacred precinct, a piece of the world protected from the profanity of the world itself. Enclosing has always been an act of foundation: a place of worship or a city is founded by enclosing it, by fencing it off from the outside.

In the modern era one of the first to rediscover the value of the enclosure, of separation from the rest in order to construct an alternative, was Mies. His Barcelona Pavilion and courtyard houses seem to have been a precise attempt to translate the sacredness of the *temenos* into modern terms. It is probably Mies we must thank for the concept of the open-air room, of elementary space that has the visual variability of the sky as its ceiling. The terrace-enclosure that Le Corbusier built for Beistégui in Paris is ironic and scenographic; in this case the open-air room substitutes the fascinating scenery of Surrealist painting for the memories of the *temenos*. The somewhat literal symbolic value of the early modern enclosures altered with the advent of the International Style. In the Breda Pavilion for the Milan Trade Fair designed by Luciano Baldassarri, the enclosure renounces the element of gravity to become a ribbon that unfolds freely like a festoon. Post-modernity rediscovered the archetypal value of the enclosure. The Fuente de los Amantes is just one example of a style of architecture, that of Louis Barragán, based totally on the principle of the enclosure and its evocative power. Nowadays all the aforementioned interpretations coexist to some extent: from open-air rooms to works of architecture composed of sequences of juxtaposed enclosures, culminating in genuine urbanistic configurations founded on the figure of the enclosure. In the case of enclosures, as often happens with non-volumetric architecture, archetypal value and spectacular effect sometimes exist side by side.

Sauerbruch Hutton

TV World Hamburg urban design for a theme park, television studios, hotel and sports world

2000
Hamburg, Germany

The project stands in an area of 320,000 m? to the south-east of Hamburg and is a theme park devoted to the world of television; a place in which to produce television and at the same time inform the public about how this is done.
The overall scheme is that of a system of enclosures or islands that are laid out around a central space. A television set is installed in the open air on each island. The enclosures are twelve metres high and are conceived as green façades formed out of rows of poplar trees or light fencing. Between the enclosures runs a continuous park that leads into the central part of the main park. The idea is for the visitor to be able to move between the enclosures as if channel-hopping on television.

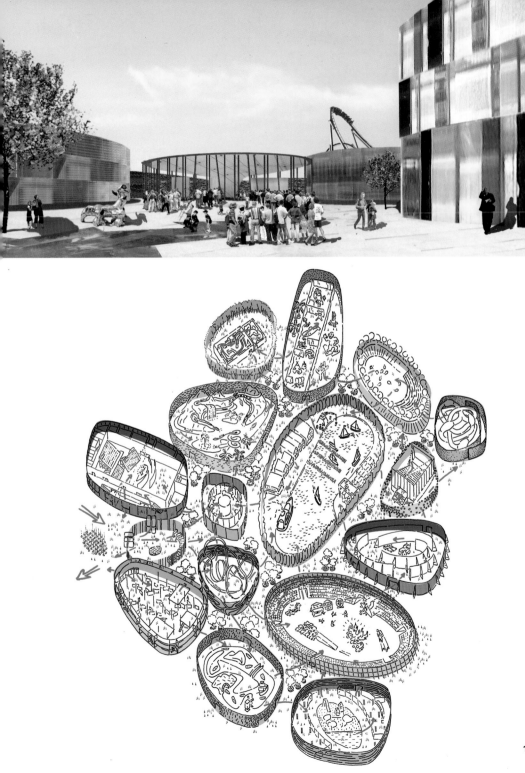

Martinez Lapeña
Elia Torres

"Ca la Llonga" Church

1974
Ibiza, Spain

The open-air church designed by Lapeña & Torres can be regarded as a succession of enclosures reduced to a series of fragments, interspersed with the surrounding nature. The distinctive feature is that the dimension of these fragments allows the original unitary design still to be perceived. The fascinating scenery can call to mind the ruins of a building found in a wood; however, this impression is countered by the rational and purist white of the walls.

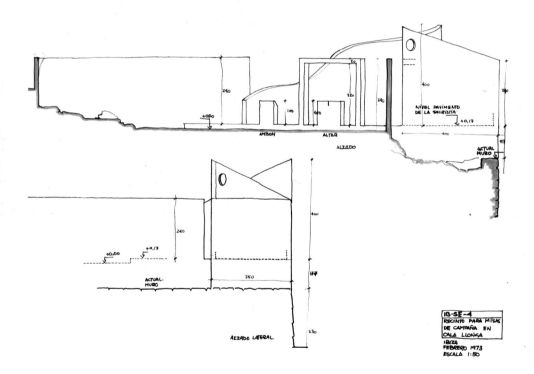

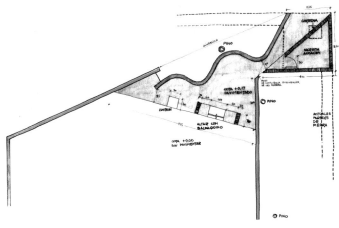

Monika Gora

Garden of Knowledge

2001
West Port in Malmö,
Sweden

The Garden of Knowledge consists of nine elements that are organized to create
an educational garden, whose theme is the relationship between nature and the
human action which modifies it. A forest of willows embraces the garden
and holds a dialogue with a number of towers arranged in a ring around the
enclosures, set at the centre of the composition. The towers are intended to
be 'castles in the air' of different heights and are constructed of steel and thatch.
The enclosures, on the other hand, house genuine naturalistic narratives, whose
aim is to involve the visitor through sensual experience.

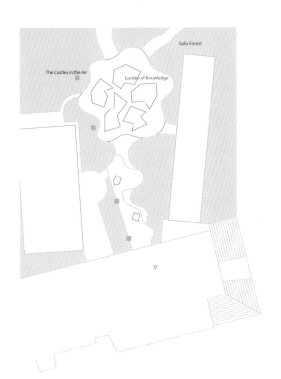

The Castles in the Air

Garden of Knowledge

Salix Forest

Carlo Scarpa
Sergio Los

IUAV Entrance, Tolentini

1966-1985
Venice, Italy

The entrance court of the University of Architecture (IUAV) harks back to the Venetian walled gardens of the past, a hypothesis that Carlo Scarpa had already explored in the garden of the Fondazione Querini Stampalia, also in Venice. The idea is that of a place able to combine the needs of a very busy public space with those of contemplation. After passing through a gateway made of sculptural objects arranged in relation to one another, a central pathway divides the two sectors, which have the appearance of two sets of scenery overturn on the ground.

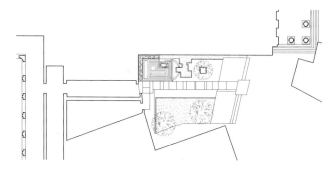

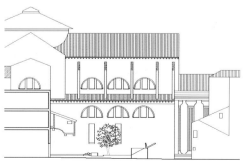

Tadao Ando   **Garden of Fine Arts**

1990-1994
Kyoto, Japan

The museum-garden of Fine Arts is located below the level of the ground so as
not to block the view of the adjoining botanical garden and is conceived as
a contemporary version of the classical Japanese garden. Images of famous
masterpieces of contemporary art, reproduced on ceramic tiles, are on display
in the museum.
The scheme of the museum-garden is that of an enclosure which embraces a
variety of plastic events: bridges, ramps, double-height structures, pools of water
and cascades. As they circulate visitors encounter a series of different sights and
vistas, in accordance with the principles of the English-style garden.

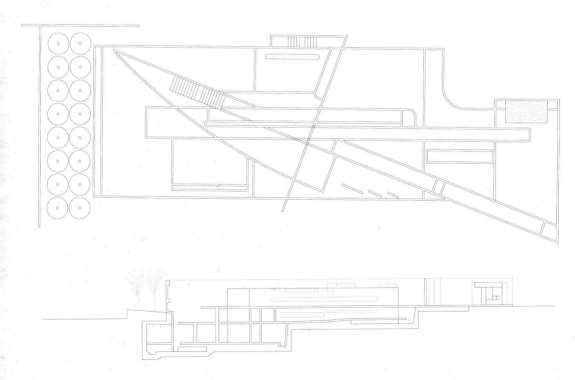

Martha Schwartz   **Whitehead Institute "Splice Garden"**

1997
Cambridge,
Massachusetts, Usa

This work by Martha Schwartz may be considered an ironic re-edition of the
famous Beistégui attic by Le Corbusier.
The garden is located on the roof of a nine-storey building and is part of an art
collection at the Whitehead Institute, a microbiological research centre.
The dimensions of the garden are restrained: 11.50 by 8.30 metres. The project
had serious limitations: no load could be placed on the roof slab and it was not
possible to irrigate any plants. Nor would it be possible to carry out any maintenance.
So the decision was taken to create a Pop scene, where the plants are obviously
fake and the arrangements of the earth look like an ironic interpretation of the Zen
garden and the French Renaissance garden.

Le Corbusier, de Beistégui
attic, Paris, 1930

Erasmian Garden

2001-2002
Rotterdam, Netherlands

The project for the Erasmian Garden was conceived to create an even more intimate and familiar space inside the park of the Arboretum Trompenburg in Rotterdam. The project consists of a pergola running along an existing canal which in turn leads to a rest area. The rest area consists of an excavation of a couple of metres below the level of the countryside, which houses the hidden garden. Against one side of it is set a pavilion whose front onto the enclosure is closed, while the one that faces onto the garden has rotating glass doors. In the case of the Erasmian Garden the figure of the enclosure is amplified by the archetypal one of the excavation.

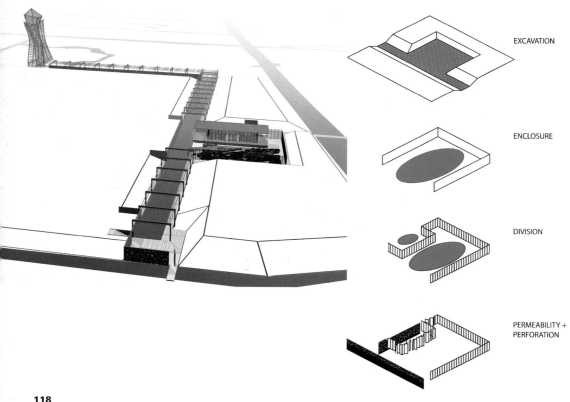

EXCAVATION

ENCLOSURE

DIVISION

PERMEABILITY +
PERFORATION

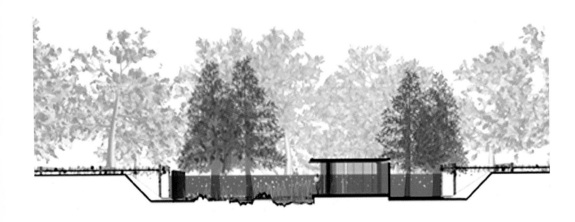

Newbern Baseball Club

2000-2001
Newbern, Hale County,
Alabama, Usa

The Newbern Baseball Club was conceived and built by students at the Rural Studio, the "department" of self-construction of the University of Alabama. The project consists of an enclosure whose configuration lends it a sculptural character. To permit the maximum visibility the chain-link fencing has no horizontal stiffening structures.

Newbern Little Wolves

2003
Newbern, Hale County,
Alabama, Usa

At Newbern Little Wolves the enclosure is made exclusively of calendered iron pipes, over which is laid a net that is the same as the one used by the catfish farmers of Alabama. In this case too the design and construction were carried out by students at the Rural Studio.

Samyn
and partners

**Totalfinaelf Europe
Service Station – Houten**

1998-1999
Houten, Netherlands

This service station is the prototype of a system developed by the designer to
commission. The theme is that of a station which could provide greater comfort
for the customer and at the same time present an efficient image. The choice,
dictated in part by the windy weather in the Netherlands, was to surround the
core of the station with a system of wings made of expanded metal. Fifty per
cent of the surface of the metal is transparent, which allows it to provide
protection from the outside without obstructing the view. Added to the set
of wings is the canopy that covers the station proper. The canopy is extremely
slender and is built out of parallel bands interspersed with cuts to let light through.

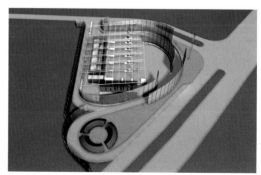

Luis Barragán   **Fuentes de Los Amantes**

1966
Los Clubes, Mexico

Barragán's architecture is an architecture of enclosures, of spaces circumscribed by walls in pastel shades whose ceiling is the Mexican sky. The manifesto of this poetics is the Fuente de Los Clubes, later renamed the Fuente de los Amantes. Set between two walls covered with magenta-coloured plaster is a basin that serves as a drinking trough for horses, which can enter without difficulty. The basin houses the two 'embracing' tree trunks, the lovers, which give the fountain its name.

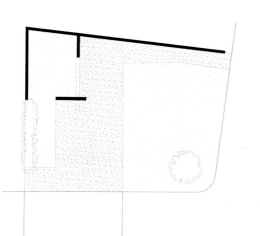

Guillermo Vázquez
Consuegra

Jardines del hospital en Valencia

1999-2001
Valencia, Spain

The proposal to plan the current gardens starts from the idea of implementing a unitary treatment for the whole landscaped space resulting from the demolition of the Hospital de los Pobres Inocentes in 1974.

This unitary action basically relies on the choice of a single type of floor and the adoption of a regulating format. A *carpet* consisting of small pieces of basaltic stone will rest on the Cartesian geometry that takes the largest element in the garden, surviving from the large-scale demolition of the hospital complex, as its benchmark.

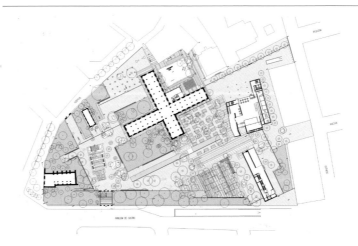

Cino Zucchi

Upgrading of the Public Spaces on Via Basso
in the Gratosoglio District

2000
Milan, Italy

The project is located in one of the large and dispersive satellite towns of Milan constructed after the war and sets itself the goal of creating a well-defined and protected place for public use. The outlines of the intervention are traced between the pre-existing structures —a farmhouse, a market, a road, a railway line— binding them together into a coherent whole. The enclosure houses a variety of objects: a wall of concrete and porphyry, a green dune, a fountain, lighting systems and furniture, to which blown-up graphic elements are added.

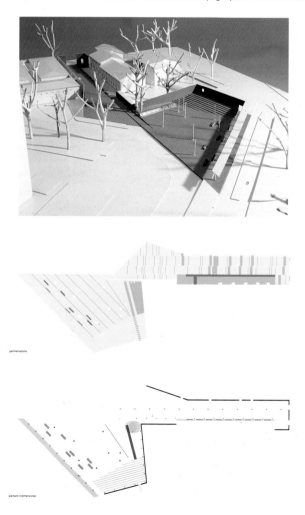

Inconsistent Vernaculars
Alberto Ferlenga

The more buildings come to resemble complicated and self-contained pieces of machinery, the more certain meanings that can be traced back to the general and simple world of timeless architecture are transferred elsewhere, into infrastructural, residual and occasional constructions, or remain confined to certain stages in their erection, vanishing as the process advances.

Thus the concrete pillars of an industrial building or a cattle shed under construction, soaring into the sky, or the spans of a highway viaduct and the heaps of earth at the edges of an excavation have, for those who are capable of going beyond the obviousness of their banality, a clearer meaning than that of the constructions to which they belong, be they common or garden warehouses or products of run-of-the-mill engineering. In those fragments of an ordinary world, the excess weight of fashions or technologies gives way to the pure and simple expression of a need. But residual memories lurk in them too, possibilities of recognition, fragments of order, that end up assigning them a role, however unwitting, and not just a presence in the increasingly agitated and confused landscapes of the contemporary world. And yet they are not true constructions, still less complete buildings, and the very will that brings them into existence is transient, often representing the fortuitous result of territorial regulations or interrupted processes, or even of automatic mechanisms linked to regular acts of maintenance. Independently of their will and thanks to the formal poverty of the world that surrounds them, rather than to their intrinsic qualities, they are the unconscious possessors of residues of character. Although condemned to a basic anonymity, they are still occasionally capable of stirring sensations that were once only produced by the best works of architecture, and that were connected with their ability to weave relations. If we were to make a list it would include the most varied types: empty spaces left over between huddles of constructions, simple impressions, mock-ups of houses built out of fleeting materials and in transient forms, earthworks, buttresses, trenches, fragments belonging to the boundless world of incompleteness, adjuncts of the road system and many others. They are materials of heterogeneous use, united by their simplicity of construction and their appearance in just a few forms, but above all by their need to be linked with something else in order for them to express any meaning. If their spread and their recurrence are often such as to determine, by themselves, the recognizability of a territory, it is in particular their programmatic lack of self-sufficiency that makes them the only visible representatives of the residual existence of relationships in a world in which works of architecture are no longer able to communicate with one another.

Often their duration is limited in time and their appearance is mutable, but it is precisely the obvious way in which they vary with the variation of the conditions that surround them that allows them to preserve a temporal dimension which seems to have totally disappeared from the majority of contemporary buildings, interested instead in endlessly prolonging an impression of newness and incorruptibility. On the other hand, if their contingent appearance changes and is subjected to continual variations, their inherently generic character, the essentiality of the materials of which they are made and their dependence on enduring necessities also makes them the only elements of permanence in areas that are changing. And, in these, their significant insubstantiality takes on guises and roles analogous to those of ruins, transforming them into ambiguous vestiges of a modern archaeology. Ruins in use we should say, meagre elements or phases in building that are not linked together by anything but the fact that they belong to a low level in the process of construction or by those formal parallels between the initial and final stages in any building. In this way they are invested with supplementary and unplanned functions with respect to the ones that determined their appearance: functions exercised with regard to the contemporary landscape that have something to do with the recognizability of its more ordinary parts and help to turn them into a sort of new vernacular. If the regular vernacular has in fact constituted, on the plane of architecture or landscape, a means of recognition of diffuse identities, derived from the sedimentation of recurrent forms linked to uses, but also to intricate processes of migration of signs, symbols and traditions, this new version of it has even more essential characteristics. Its force is due more to the direct experience of whoever encounters it than to any iconography but, as happens with all types of vernacular, its connection with the location is closer than what most buildings today are capable of establishing, and this is the aspect that makes it more interesting.

They are, nevertheless, *works of architecture without architects* and not even endowed with the beauty or historical significance of the examples gathered by Bernard Rudofsky. They cannot even be said to present the precursory characteristics that Werner Lindner attributed to the pieces catalogued by themes in his invaluable little volumes, a source of inspiration for many modern architects. In this case, they are for the most part nondescript and unobtrusive, leftovers rather than forerunners. Their importance emerges in negative and is inversely proportional, as has been said, to the relational capacities of the architecture of our time, unable to transfer quality from itself to the space in which it is set. Perhaps we cannot even speak of importance seeing that, in the case in question, there would be considerable difficulties in defining their characteristics objectively in terms of unambiguous qualities. Let us say rather that in this world of pieces, traces and instants, they constitute a realm in which we still perceive the presence of several possibilities linked to the production of the diffuse values that bind together architecture and territory, and that it is more from their typical absence of substance than from their obvious characteristics that these possibilities spring. They can be seen, and this would be desirable, as a mine of forms and modes of being to be moulded and interpreted, or they can be ignored, but it is not possible to avoid running into them and noticing their active presence where everything seems to assert its isolation and separateness and nothing else appears to be capable of holding together the variegated fragments of the shattered landscapes in which we live.

Olivo Barbieri,
A4 Milano-Vicenza

Louis I. Kahn, Sketch
of a Civic Center, from
the essay "Monumentality",
1944

Design

Immediately after the war, Louis Kahn proposed a design
for a civic centre in which a canopy on a monumental scale
characterized an institutional and representative public space.
In this case what we are dealing with could be defined as
non-volumetric design. By this term is meant an architectural
project that utilizes the principles and methods of industrial
design, lingering over an accurate definition of the object in
such a way as to elevate the latter to the state of an element
characterizing the surrounding space. Non-volumetric design
is a typical product of public space; in fact if we were to try
to line up the objects of non-volumetric design of recent
decades, we would obtain a genuine narrative, a sequence
indicative of how public space is evolving.
On a reduced scale non-volumetric design produces elements
of lighting and seats, but distancing itself from street furniture
inasmuch as it conceives these elements outside of their specific
functionality, as genuine aesthetic presences capable of grabbing
attention. Even on a minute scale, non-volumetric design does
not renounce the monumental component to be found
in the aforementioned designs of Louis Kahn, adding to this
an ever more present expressionism of Pop derivation. On the
intermediate scale non-volumetric design realizes footbridges
and works of architecture of a moderate size, but always with
a powerful visual impact. From a technical point of view
non-volumetric design is characterized in general by a certain
indifference to the scale of intervention, proposing conceptually
similar configurations independently of the dimensions.
Another distinctive characteristic is the way that it interposes
itself between architecture, design and sculpture.

Acconci Studio   **Möbius Bench**

2000-2001
Fukuroi City, Japan

The plastic seat is designed along the lines of the famous Möbius strip: a Y-shaped section that forms the seat rotates and turns back on itself like a screw. The design is intended to permit a varied use of the seat. People can sit on it in the normal way, inside or outside the spiral, or lie on it, or it can be turned into a plaything for children. The Möbius seat can be thought of as a sculptural piece of street furniture, a presence in urban space that makes itself felt above and beyond the functions of seating or lighting.

EMBT
Enric Miralles,
Benedetta Tagliabue

Banco Lungomare para Escofet

1998-1999
Barcellona, Spagna

The 'Lungomare' seat/deckchair has a form that resembles a solidified piece of sea, an example of organic design which permits a use that its authors describe as 'many-coloured' and above all sets out to blend in with its natural surroundings, while remaining a surprise for anyone who comes across it.

Monika Gora   **Common Ground**

2001-2002
Umeå, Sweden

This sculptural object is conceived to create a continuity that is more than visual between an external courtyard and the hall of the Hospital of Umeå University. The sculptures are all of the same form, but made of two different materials: black stone or polyester reinforced with glass fibre and dyed a magenta colour, illuminated with fluorescent lamps from the inside. In the intentions of the designer, the form of the objects has a metaphorical meaning, halfway between a sofa, a heart and a flower.

Sean Godsell
Architects

Park Bench House

2002
Melbourne, Australia

In Melbourne, which is considered one of the most liveable cities in the world,
173 out of every 10,000 people are homeless. The Park Bench House is intended
to provide the simplest and cheapest form of shelter for the needy. At the same
time the shelter can be turned into a bench in the daytime. The bench/shelter
is a clear example of the current tendency to design multi-functional and fitting
objects for public space that are sensitive to new social requirements.

Bicycle – Parking Lot and Guardhouse

2000
Den Haag,
Netherlands

A rectangular bicycle parking lot has been created between a large car park, an outdoor bowling rink and a swimming pool. The project consists of a suspended structure, a spiral ramp that rises from the ground and winds between the existing trees. At the top of the ramp is set the booth of the parking lot, a projecting sphere that lights up at night, becoming a landmark for the area. The ramp, by contrast, is illuminated from below with soft light.
The general idea is to make the simple act of parking a bicycle an experience that is no longer banal and mechanical, but an eccentric act which allows its owner to live for a moment in the crown of the trees and see an anonym place from another point of view.

Aldo Aymonino,
Seste Engineering

Observation tower in Venice Lagoon

2004
Venice, Italy

On the north quay of the Bocca di Chioggia is set a large belvedere, a genuine machine for leisure in the open air. It has the appearance of a huge roof supported by a series of concrete and iron structures that differ from one another.
The large belvedere provides shade from the sun and, by means of a continuous wooden ramp, takes visitors to a height of 9,00 metres above sea level, from where they can enjoy a view of the landscape of the Venetian lagoon.

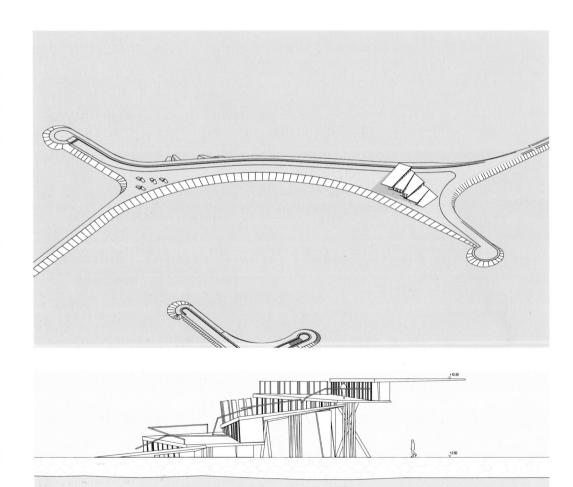

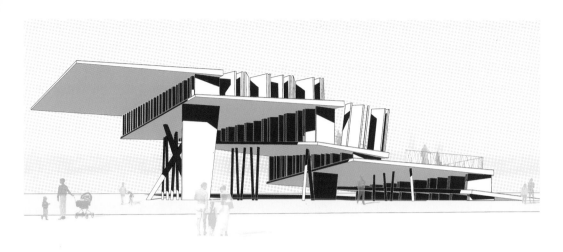

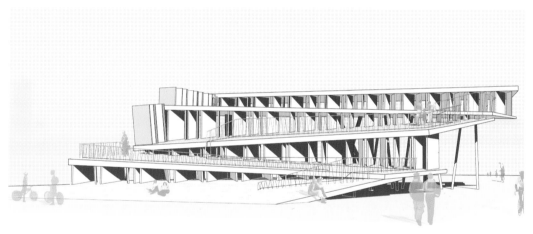

Studio Granda

Höfdabakka Highway Interchange

1994-1995
Reykjavik, Iceland

The project for the Höfdabakka Highway Interchange can be seen as an experiment in the application of industrial design to infrastructure, in this case a junction between a motorway and a road above it carrying less traffic. The bridge is 37 m long and varies in width from 35 to 60 m. The spindle-shaped columns supporting the deck are made of coloured steel with a Y-section and establish a dialectical contrast with the plastic solidity of the concrete deck.

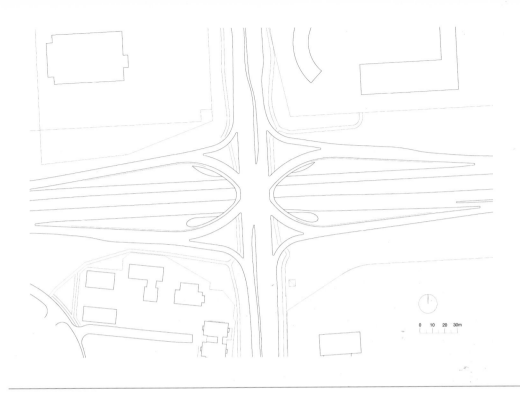

0   10   20   30m

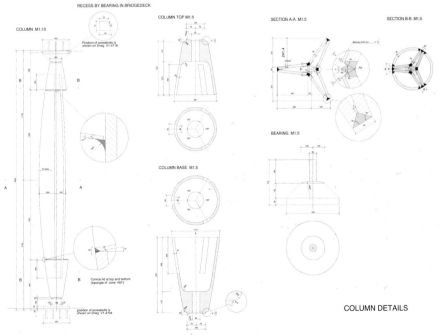

RECESS BY BEARING IN BRIDGEDECK

COLUMN. M1:10

Position of screwbolts is
shown on Drwg. V1-4716

COLUMN TOP M1:5

SECTION A-A. M1:5

SECTION B-B. M1:5

BEARING. M1:5

COLUMN BASE. M1:5

Conical lid at top and bottom
(topangle of cone 160°)

position of screwbolts is
shown on Drwg. V1-4704

COLUMN DETAILS

151

Studio Granda   **Kringlumyra Bridge**

1995
Reykjavik, Iceland

The Kringlumyra Bridge is a footbridge spanning a motorway and linking together two parts of the town. The long and sinuous bridge has a section that projects outwards from the girder that runs along one side. A parapet consisting of a coloured grating protects users of the footbridge from the traffic below and the cold north wind.

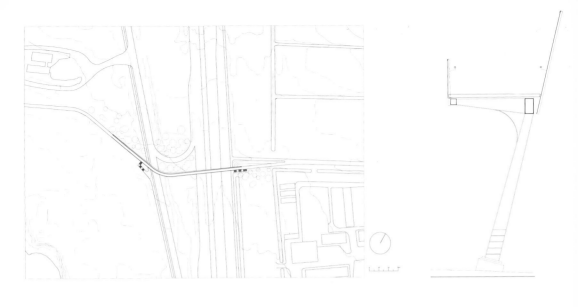

Outdoor Installation, "Dunescape"

2000
Long Island City,
NY, Usa

The installation is designed to give people an opportunity to enjoy the summer on Long Island sitting on the platform, lying in the sun or the shade, strolling in the little pool among cool sprays of water. It consists of a continuous wooden structure made up of over 6000 cedar planks that houses a series of elements such as sunshades, a hut and deckchairs, etc. The structure is mobile; when pulled upwards it provides shelter from the sun, but when it is on the ground is takes the form of seats at different heights. When pulled to one side it becomes a wall that contains cabins for changing; when laid totally flat it turns into a dance floor.

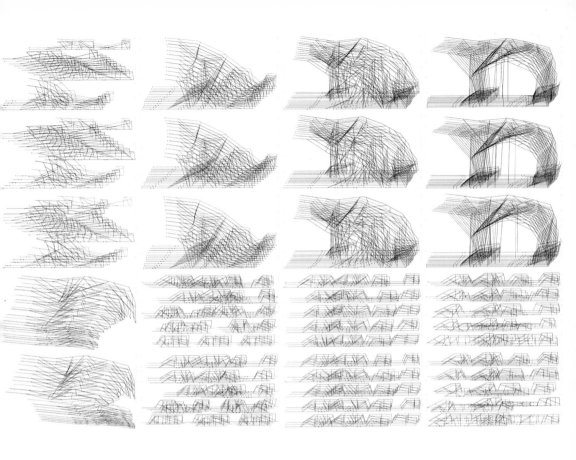

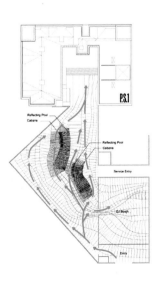

Walkway at the Imperial Fora

1999-2005
Rome, Italy

The walkway has been constructed in the archaeological area of the Roman Forum and has been given a character that underlines its distance from the archaeological area, avoiding any mimicry. The walkway is built entirely out of Cor-Ten steel and runs along the walls. To emphasize the contrast with the massive thickness of the Roman masonry, the catwalk consists of a surface that bends, offering a silent comment on the surrounding ruins. The weathered surface of the Cor-Ten helps to further underline this intention on the part of the designers.

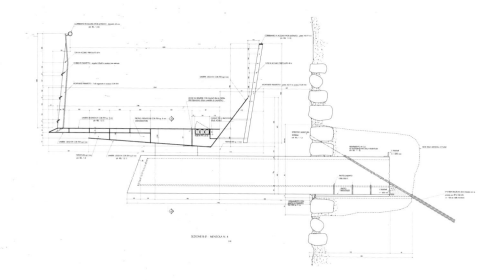

Reality and Architecture: Totality and Dissolution of the Object
Ilhyun Kim

At the threshold of the object

"Simultaneity of the environment, dislocation, dismantlement of objects, dispersion and fusion of parts, all liberated from common logic and independent from one another": with these words Umberto Boccioni had described his work "La strada entra in casa", displayed at the Futurist Ex1hibition at the Bernheim-Juene Gallery in Paris in 1912[1]. The title itself exemplifies the notion of the environment and the atmosphere that Boccioni, Sant'Elia and other Italian futurists had attempted to recreate, focused on a fusion between body, architecture and infrastructure, as "all that is solid melts into air". This synthesis was later to be that sought by cabarets, by total theatre, perfectly recreated in the sets of Metropolis, where an atmosphere of conflict, of pleasure and anxiety, precision and spontaneity, progress and desperation was breathed. Another revolution of the futurists, as regards the relationships between parts, is the involvement of the spectator, now accomplished increasingly intimately and directly, in search of an empathic, finally authentic aesthetic experience. What the futurists sought was therefore a moral transparency in the relations between the environment, the art object and the observer, an ontological whole. Now, even if the objects could have proven anomalous, it is prcisely according to their anomalousness that they could manifest their capacity for an involvement beyond the observer's expectations. This is when, therefore, the meaning of the open work was clarified for the futurists, that is, an incomplete work as it is, in constant expectation of the involvement of the surrounding environment and the spectator.

The futurist ontological revolution remains to this day. Minimalism has in fact replaced the dynamism of the object with staticity, but the relations between the parts are ultimately the same as for futurism[2]. In both cases a sculpture, whether dynamic or static, is at the same time a magnet and a mirror. A magnet as it succeeds in attracting the fluctuating meaning of things, a mirror as it invites the observer to meditate on himself and on his own prejudices. It is precisely this ambiguity, from which the multiplicity of meanings comes about, that is the salient quality of these objects, whether futurist or minimal; works conceived, therefore, to prompt a perceptive and intellectual reaction.

The architectural objects of the public space underlie the same ontological rules of futurist and minimal sculpture. The reason for these objects travels substantially along two channels: on one hand, the permanence of the same, on the other, its mask, its aspect "for the occasion". Most times the mask prevails over the more intimate reasons and the reasons of the object are expressed as signs and codes of an instant, as pure communi-

cation[3]. It was on these principles that Christo, Matta Clark and Whiteread worked, on how the ontological involvement of the observer could be exported to the architectural dimension, thus acquiring other meanings, more linked to the concept of the object or the public space[4]. These artists then sought a social implication in artistic action and did so by proposing works with a strong and substantial social implication, denying the permanence of works as a coercive expression of power, as it is precisely transience that is the the quality necessary for a work to guarantee a multiplicity of meanings and therefore to be democratic. Matta-Clark states: "Our thinking about anarchitetture was more elusive than doing pieces that would demonstrate an alternative attitude to buildings, or, rather to the attiudes that determine containerization of usable space. These attitudes are very deep-set... Architecture is environment too. When you're living in the city, the whole fabric is architectural in some sense. We were thinking more about metaphoric voids, gaps, leftover spaces, places that were not developed". This affirmation overlaps with Boccioni's statement of 1914[5].

Situations and Realities

Far from being an ideal synthesis of art and science, architecture continuously confronts the crisis of reference shifting within history, nature and technology. The synthesis of arts, the will to form, the total work of art, and empathy, each proposition privileges a different centre of gravity in the field of architecture. Meditation on the notion of place in the historical avant-gardes is double folded and complementary of atopia and dystopia. The same thing could be affirmed for the notion of the object-subject between formal autonomy and empirical experience.

The lyrical artificial landscape of the picturesque and the terrifying overwhelming one of the sublime, distance and dimension are once again crucial elements for understanding the relations between parts[6]. The appraisal of the building in agony and decay in Romanticism merges with the sense of terror emaned by Piranesi's Carceri. In the artificial landscape of panoramas, incisions, painting, that represented on maps, photographs, the distinction between the natural and the artificial vanishes. Hence it becomes a matter of recognizing the artificiality of architecture, in the world of man-made objects, and —as Alberti bitterly admitted— its inherent destructive character against nature.

Alberto Burri's Cretto in Gibellina (1981), a great environmental work of art, is at the opposite of the Romantic idea of the dissolution of form, as the object becomes the medium for both the remembrance of tragedy and the persistence of collective memory. Size does matter, but not in the case of Aldo Rossi's Teatro del Mondo (1979), a travelling object condensed with historical reminiscence, which nevertheless has its ephemeral destiny. Rossi's work in fact perfectly represents the conceptual expansion of the image obtained through the condensation of its significance. On one hand, in Burri's case, the physical duration, the ancient one of monuments, is a priority; monuments that are the embodiment of collective memories, and on the other, the ephemeral and the dissolution of the object that the ephemeral aspires to impose, as a symbol of the temporality of experience.

An architectural object, as an aesthetic and social device, is called upon to respond to complex exigencies in the contemporary. It is not casual that the debates on superstructure and anonymous architecture emerge at the same time. Architecture without architects is an extreme warning to recognize the socio-cultural value of lesser architecture, to denounce the falsity of planning, but stressing the social figure of the architect, the authenticity and sincerity of form, and the aspiration of total transformation[8].

The relationship between the object and the subject is not static, as Moholy Nagy had proposed on the subject of perception in terms of parallax, with Vision in Motion(8). With the concept of parallax, he indicates the mutual consequences of perception between the observer and the ambience.

As we have understood learning from Las Vegas and seing the view from the road, it is not specific urban facts related with the placeness of these, but rather the attitude that enables us to evaluate the daily cityscape and the man-made environment. With the stratification of the different layers of time, or the contemporary stratification of fragments compressed in what we call present, modernity is neither history nor chronology, but the consciousness of temporality.

Wandering in the city, getting lost purposely, has been fundamental to encounters with the ever-changing aspects and unexpected experience that the city offers constantly. This occurs not just to Benjamin's Paris or Berlin but everywhere, as one drifts within a palimpsest of episodes and events. Probably the worst enemy of contemporary existence is still boredom and habit, as Baudelaire had stated. Probably neither a dandy nor a fleneur are more creative users of the urban space compared to a beggar, with his art of survival, with his instinctive application of Nolli's mapping, thanks to the misery granted by modern planning in the last half-century. Distancing itself from zoning, pre-established circulations and determined usage, the city becomes a place of arbitrary drift and discovery. Although not totally deprived of revolutionary ideals, a city is still a spontaneous place of occupation and festivity. Almost as a tactic of guerrilla warfare, clubs and rave parties, similar to the oldest collective rituals, but filled with new technological effects and primitive stimuli, occupy abandoned and peripheral zones of the city.

A series of contemporary research projects, such as "Tour of the Monuments of Passaic New Jersey" (1967), a field trip to the huge industrial complex in the Ruhr district of Germany (1968), the reportage in Yucatan, especially Hotel Palenque (1969-1972) are not secondary with respect to the humanist tradition of voyage and treatises written in search of certainties and ideals that occurred in antiquity.

With a fetishistic, peeping attitude, impatient zapping, there emerges not just a crisis of attention but a different situation related with the architectural object. Mobility and stillness are not dialectic, but two aspects of the same state of being of the object. Two emblematic devices – the Internet and the mobile phone – enable individuals to relate to the world of information and experience. If the Internet provides "travel without moving" and chance encounters online in atopia, the mobile phone enables an individual to exercise his or her presence in different physical places at the same time, finally achieving once forbidden ubiquitousness.

Urbanscape as a "Total work of art"

Rosalind Krauss, in her essay "Sculpture in the expanded field" diagnosed the conceptual evolution of sculpture, when Minimalism seemed to have concluded its cycle, by the end of the seventies[9]. Then the object-sculpture seemed to devour every possible material, multiplying its boundaries everywhere. In this situation we wondered what the status of architecture and its 'territory' could be.

After more than twenty years, it is not hazardous to say that the scenery of the current architectural discipline faces similar but more drastic changes, as different concepts such as mutation, contamination, disjunction, shift, are now an integral part of the process of identification. Those who still firmly believe in the purity of architecture as a teaching discipline and in the defense of academic ideals might be disturbed by what actually occurs daily. But before filtering with the pre-established dogmas, it is worthwhile to take a glance without prejudice at the realities where often words are not enough to seize their intrinsic dynamics.

The relationship between an artistic object and its environment had been fully dealt by the historical avant-gardes and later in the 1960s. The artistic object was considered as a battlefield of representation and perception, a place of opposition of the continuous en-counter in which we identify traces of the twofold process of dissolution and reconstruction along its threshold[10]. In effect, the definition itself of the object, a thing that has properties and relations, already indicates the conflict status with and within reality.

If the ideal of bourgeois culture was to produce objects that could educate the tastes of the consumer and represent image-types, applied art and design objects were called upon to mediate the loss of identity determined by the new industrial paradigm[11]. Although sharing the belief in the potentiality of objecthood, the aspiration of the historical avant-gardes was to create a whole new environment along with revolution, considering art as a potential vehicle to transform society and to convert the masses into new beings.

An object, whether as an envelope in the pre-established context or as a sole structure presuming the tabula rasa, consequently oscillates its meaning, yet at the same time establishing a new relationship with reality. As a Gesamtkunstwerk, a total work of art, outside of the confines of theatricality, whether as an ideal collaboration of artists or the creation of a whole environment, the role to renew reality is once again given to the object of art, understood as an object of affection, objet trouvé, readymade, representation of exotic primitivism or the fetishism of Surrealism; in all these cases there is an evident criticism of the consumption of commodities and more in general of the notion of the art object. The strategy thus becomes that of resistance with satire and irony against the reification of the capitalist market. Each of these is an attempt to transform the nature of man and society through the elevation of the art object to a social catalyst of the cultural revolution.

It is not casual that, returning from the desert after finishing the Spiral Jetty, Smithson called New York an urban desert. At the extreme but with the same spirit of mind, Christo and Jeanne Claude, while preparing a major object installation in Central Park, were asked if the work was their biggest, their answer was simple: "there are bigger works of art, such as bridges, buildings and airports". By this they meant that each of these "man-made objects" is per se a huge Gesamtkunstwerk, where most human activities take place[12].

The exercise of critical awareness and the adequate initiatives inherent in this would bring about an alternative urban usage otherwise cancelled out by the regulations of institutional planning. Absence and the ephemeral are not negativity, but the presence of indescribable essence.

If architecture is simply defined as a permanent construction, it will be incapable of responding to the diverse and capricious exigencies of the contemporary metropolitan individual. The cross-breeding of objects and materials, the heterogeneity of types and the contamination of genres are only a small part of the many tactics to discover the new status of architecture, which must be far removed from the mono-functional blocks indicated by building codes. The occasional discovery and the chance encounter of destinies occur daily in the publicity of urban spaces such as courts and pavilions, or better yet, such as social containers and platforms. Like the Buddhist temples in the midst of nature in Oriental landscape paintings, urban voids are neither residual nor excremental, but potential fragments of contemplation and obsession.

The notion of "Unvolumetric architecture" in this publication not only proposes a critical category regarding the current multi-valences of contemporary architectural objects and interventions, but even attempts to retrace an alternative epistemological basis for the theories and history of architecture. An architectural object, disregarding its physical size, may extend, generating situations and creating the sensation of placeness, and at the same time it may contract, creating a unicum where multiple significances and experiences overlap. An architectural object, in its movement between totality and dissolution through objecthood, between field and situation, that of the modern, wanders within the labyrinth of images, things and words. An object matters if architecture embraces the entire atmosphere in which human activities are engaged. After the resolute declaration of failure, the old manifesto of the historical avant-gardes re-emerges like a ghost: "everything is art and everyone is an artist".

[1] Regarding the research by Boccioni, see also the following works: *Visioni simultanee*, 1911, oil on canvas, 60.5 x 60.5 cm, Von der Heydt-Museum, Wuppertal; *Elasticità*, 1912, oil on canvas, 100 x 100 cm, Civico Museo d'Arte Contemporanea (CIMAC); *Testa+casa+luce*, 1911-1912 (destroyed); *Sviluppo di una bottiglia nello spazio*, 1912, Bronze, h. 38 cm, 1912.; *Forme uniche della continuità nello spazio*, 1913, bronze, 112 x 40 x 90 cm , Civiche Raccolte d'Arte di Milano.

[2] C. Greenberg, "Recentness of Sculpture", in ed. Gregory Battcock, *Minimal Art: A Critical Anthology*, Dutton, New York 1968 (1967), pp. 180-186; M. Michael, "Art and Objecthood", *Artforum*, Summer 1967. To these criticisms, the responses are quite simple and clear. Frank Stella states: "What you see is what you see" and Donald Judd writes: "A shape, a volume, a colour, a surface is something itself". One might also recall a famous saying by Oscar Wilde: "the mystery of the world is the visible, not the invisible". See the recent study by H.Foster, *The Return of the Real: Art and Theory at the End of the Century*, October Books, MIT Press, Cambridge, Mass. 1996.

[3] The works referred to here are the following: Christo & Jeanne Claude, *The wall-wrapped, Via Vittorio Veneto e Villa Borghese* 1974; G. Matta Clark, *Splitting* 1974; R. Whiteread, *The House, 193 Grove Road in Bow, E3, East London* 1993. The previous works of Man Ray (*The Riddle* or *The Enigma of Isidore Ducasse* 1920.), Bruce Nauman (*Space under My Steel Chair in Dusseldorf*, 1965-68) and Lucio Fontana (*Concetti Spaziali*, 1951-) are also to be considered.

[4] *Ibidem*.

[5] "Every place must be excellent for us to work and everything must be material of creation that is not exterior and narrative, but interior and interpretative". U.Boccioni, *Pittura e scultura futuriste*, SE, Milan 1997 (1914), p. 19.

[6] C. Ginzburg, *Occhiali di legno: Nove riflessioni sulla distanza*, Feltrinelli, Milan 1998.

[7] The emergence of the so-called Utopia International, to mention, among many, Superstudios, Archigram and Japanese Metabolisms, oscillates between these two extremes. B.Rudofsky, *Architecture without Architects. A short Introduction to Non-Pedigreed Architecture*, Doubleday, New York 1964.

[8] "Vision in motion is a synonym for simultaneity and space-time; a means to comprehend the new dimension. Vision in motion also signifies planning, the projective dynamics of our visionary faculties", in L. Moholy Nagy, *Vision in Motion*, Hillison & Etten, Chicago 1947, p. 12.

[9] R. Krauss, "Sculpture in the expanded field", October, no. 8, Spring 1979.

[10] Ibid., p. 366.

[11] W. Benjamin, "Experience and Poverty" (1934), *Selected Writings*, Vol. 2, Harvard University Press, Cambridge, MA 1996-2003, pp. 731-735 ; A. Loos, "My Poor Little Rich Man" in *Spoken into the Void: Collected Essays 1897-1900*, Opposition Books (MIT Press) 1987.

[11] Hence the distance between minimal sculptures and relatively minute objects in the vast landscape is quite subtle. Opposite to the hyper-enlargement of the banal object of Claes Oldenburg, but with identical intentions, lies the testimony of Robert Smithson: "A crack in the wall, if viewed in terms of scale, not size, could be called the Grand Canyon". But the contribution of Land Art is not confined in the realm of perception, but more radically the notion of place as reality itself". T.W. Adorno, *Aesthetic Theory*, Routledge & Kegan, London 1984 (1970), p. 253.

Fishing trabocco
in the Adriatic Sea

Shelte

Providing shelter is the primary responsibility of architecture. Even before they were given walls, in fact, roofs, shelters were erected. Even today the abbé Laugier's well-known image of the rustic hut can still be considered the icon that best reflects the attraction of modern thought to the primitive construction, necessary, functional and, as such, 'true'. It was the avant-garde movements that made primitivism the fundamental characteristic of a radically renewed aesthetics, which ceased to look to the recent past only to fall under the spell of the remote, still uncivilized past. Then the icon became the overhang: a thin slab that indicates and protects the entrances of buildings, turning them into welcoming and receptive public places. So is no accident that cantilever roofs appear in Tony Garnier's evocative plans for the Cité Industrielle, in the utopian designs of a city functional to its own time, conceived for the production and movement of goods and people, and therefore in need of large, sheltered public spaces. From Garnier onwards the canopy was raised to the status of symbol of an architectural language that, although transformed over almost a century of existence, is still fascinated by the overhang. From this perspective we can consider the kiosk or stand a fitted canopy, whose function goes beyond that of the temporary and emergency shelter.

The *trabocchi* or fish traps of the Adriatic Sea are kiosks on piles, built over time by fishermen. In these unusual constructions the concept of fitted shelter is very clear, composed out of whatever salvaged materials came to hand, above and beyond any kind of pre-established form.

Onl Oosterhuis
Lénárd

Oak leaf shaped sculpture functions as band stand

1997
Oldemarkt
Vijverbos, Netherlands

A sketch of an oak leaf by Ilona Lénárd inspired the form of the Music Sculptures. The stand/sculpture was made in the workshop from steel and faced with sheet steel varying in thickness from 3 to 5 mm and sprayed green. The structure was then cut into three pieces and assembled in the park, on the banks of the pond over which it projects for a length of two metres. The sculpture, which can be folded back on itself, is used as a stand for music and for dance performances.

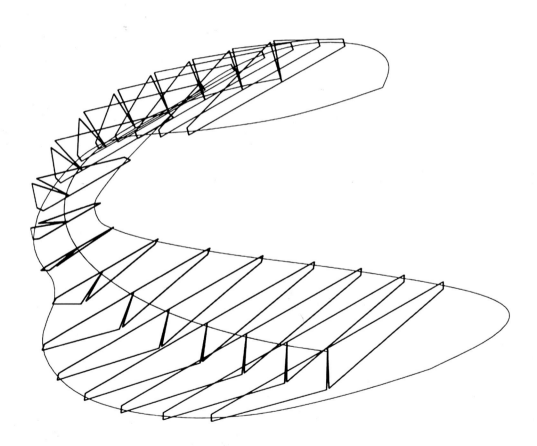

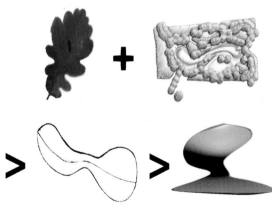

Níall Mc Laughlin
Architects

Bandstand

2002
De la Warr Pavillon
Grounds, Bexhill,
UK

The design of this stand, intended to house various events, was produced by the
architect in collaboration with students at a series of workshops. The form derives
from computerized analysis of the propagation of sound. The stand is made
of coated fibreglass and rests on steel bases.

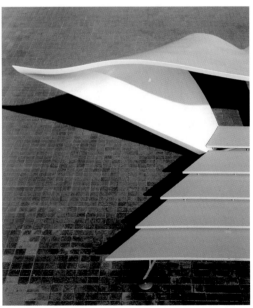

EMBT
Enric Miralles,
Benedetta Tagliabue

Pergola University Campus in Vigo

1999-2003
Vigo, Spain

The pergola of the campus of Vigo University is part of a larger project for the new entrance to the campus, which will entail the layout of sports facilities, car parks and urbanized areas, and finally the construction of new buildings. The various interventions will be linked together by an extensive programme of reforestation. In this connection, the designers speak of a phase of 'quasi-urban' densification, obtained through light architectural signs which will be replaced in the medium term by the reforestation. In the light of this intention the long and continuous pergola can be regarded as a feature in which the artificial and natural aspects of the project are brought together.

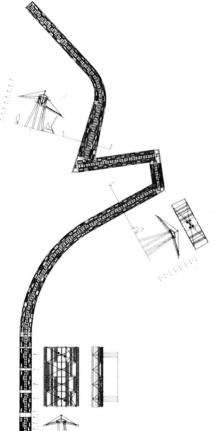

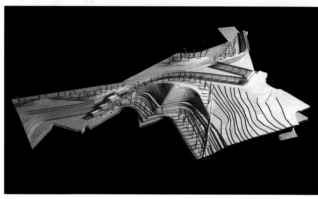

Shuhei Endo

Springtecture Orléans

2000
Orléans, France

The architecture of Shuhei Endo tends to refer to one figure in particular, created by folding simple notched sheets of metal on themselves. In this sense the Springtecture Orléans project can be considered the concept of a poetics, in this case applied to the theme of the ephemeral pavilion.

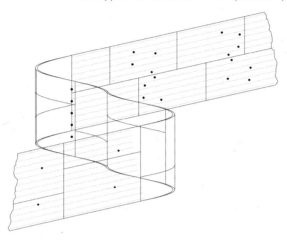

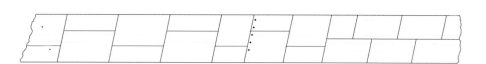

Halftecture F

1996-1997
Fukui City, Japan

Halftecture F is a band of notched and galvanized sheet metal that runs parallel to a railway line and is supported by a simple row of standardized pillars. At the end the band turns back on itself, creating a rest area. All the elements of the design are cheap and easy to find on the market.

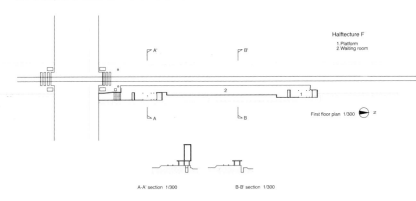

Halftecture F

1. Platform
2. Waiting room

First floor plan 1/300

A-A' section 1/300   B-B' section 1/300

East elevation 1/300

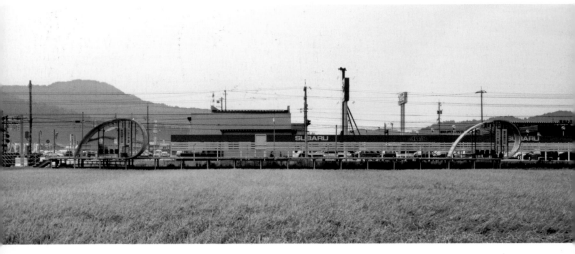

Rural Studio

Cedar pavillon

2001-2002
Perry County,
Alabama, Usa

The cedar pavilion is tucked in amongst the trees and engages with an old picnic area which was made in the 1930s. The ceiling soars to seven meters at its highest point, while the floor surface wraps up to form benches and make a formal entryway ramp. The entire floor surface is made of cedar which was donated by a local community member.
The students cut the trees out of a cedar thicket, took them to be milled into lumber and then erected the pavilion.

Marpillero - Pollak
architects

Thresholds of Eibs Pond Park

2003
Staten Island, NY, Usa

The project uses design strategies to integrate urban social and ecological issues
with restoration of a 17 acre freshwater wetland park in an underserved urban
neighborhood. It focuses on an ecologically disturbed three-acre parcel along the
southern boundary of the park. As shown in the diagram of Preliminary Design
Criteria, storm water management, circulation, and programming are deployed
to address issues of perimeter control and public safety. Street end parks replace
dead ends at two local entrances, connecting to a boardwalk, which is the central
element of the design, linking dead-end paths and severed sidewalks.

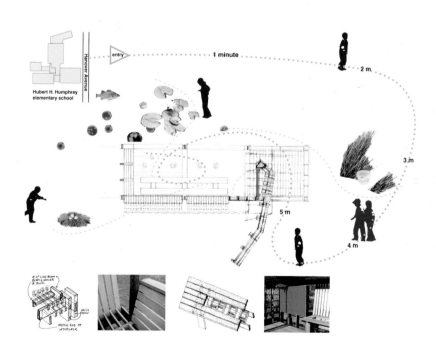

Flower Power

1998-2002
Schiphol
Haarlemmermeer
Haarlem, Netherlands

Flower Power is the name given to a series of interventions aimed at upgrading the Dutch system of public road transport. The project consists in the design of a series of typological elements such as light roofs, parapets, visual and sound barriers, facings, areas of paving, etc., which, in order to adapt to the different conditions, envisage a series of variations on the theme. All fourteen bus stops are black and white, with the exception of the roof of coloured glass. The bicycle tunnel at Haarlemmermeer represented here is also in the typical Dutch colour of orange.

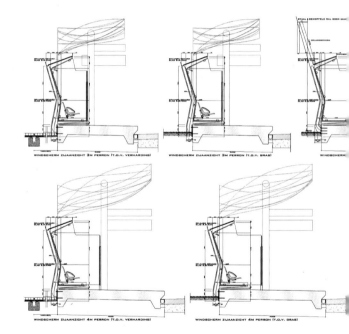

Fluid Vehicle – The Amazing Whale Jaw

1999-2003
Hoofddorp, Netherlands

The Amazing Whale Jaw is a filling station for buses situated in front of a hospital. It was the designers' intention for the overall form to follow Oscar Niemeyer's teachings about an architecture halfway between early 'white' modernism and the 'black' baroque. More in general, this object, whose appearance and technology are increasingly distant from those of traditional architecture, can be regarded as one of the most radical expressions of 'blob design'. The building is made entirely of synthetic materials and its dimensions of fifty by ten by five metres make it the largest structure in the world to be built of these materials. It was constructed in its entirety in the workshop and then assembled on site.

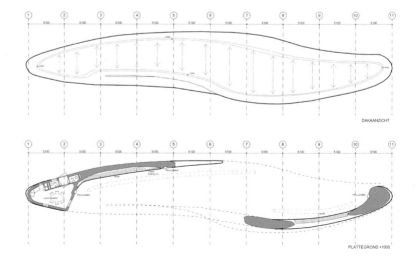

OOSTAANZICHT

WESTAANZICHT

DOORSNEDE STRAMIEN 4

DOORSNEDE STRAMIEN 9

NOORDAANZICHT

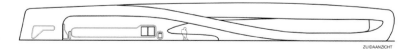

ZUIDAANZICHT

189

Francesco Cellini
Eugenio Cipollone

Layout of the Area of the Basilica of San Paolo fuori le mura in Rome

1999
Rome, Italy

The design for the roofing of the Sepolcreto Ostiense is part of a broader programme for the layout of the area of the basilica of San Paolo fuori le Mura in Rome. The roof that used to cover the exhibits has been replaced by a new structure measuring 37 x 18 m. This consists of a slender, lowered vault of constant curvature, faced on the outside with oxidised sheet copper.

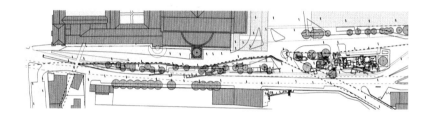

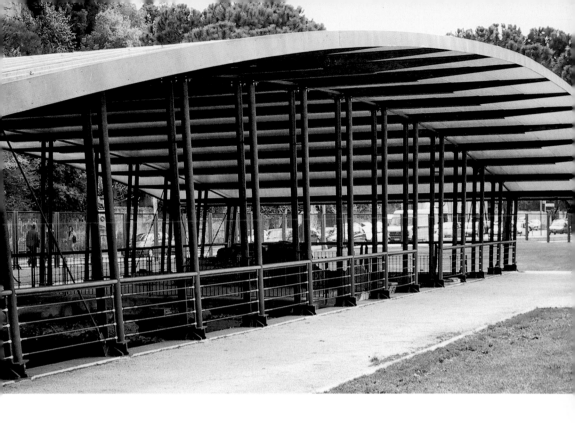

Francesco Cellini
Eugenio Cipollone
Maria Margarita Segarra
Maria Lagunes

Layout of the Roman theatre of Spoleto

2005
Spoleto, Italy

For the rehabilitation of the Roman theatre of Spoleto the decision was taken to intervene by fragments, in an effort not to pervert the archaeological nature of the site. The project focuses on several points: a new loggia, the reclamation of the stage and cavea and the routes. The new loggia has the appearance of a memory of the Middle Ages drawn from the pictures of Giotto. Opposite the balconies of the loggia runs a suspended system where the lighting panels slide on tracks.

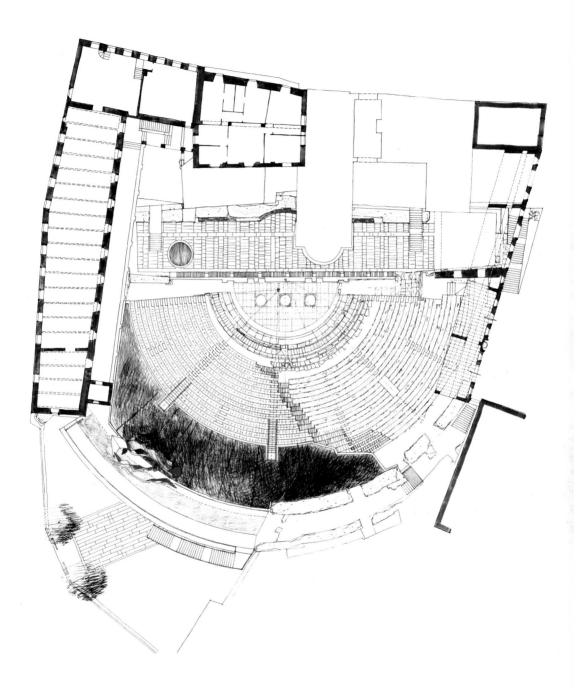

Stanford University Modular Shelters

1996
Stanford University
Palo Alto Campus,
California, Usa

This modular shelter is conceived as a flexible kiosk to be set up on the campus of Stanford University and, combined in several different ways, can be used as a bus stop, a kiosk for rest, an open-air bar or, in its vertical configuration, a screen for projections. The materials are lacquered steel and concrete. The kiosk is intended to be an object halfway between the primitive hut and a mechanical device, and the different functions that it is able to house can be obtained through minimal adjustments to the basic module.

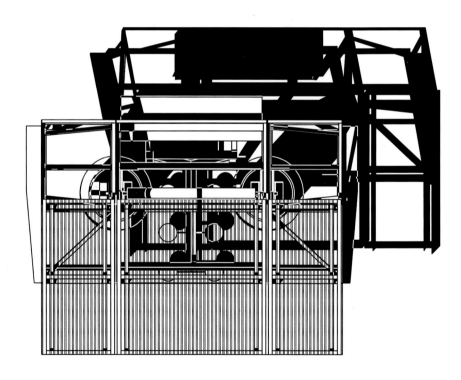

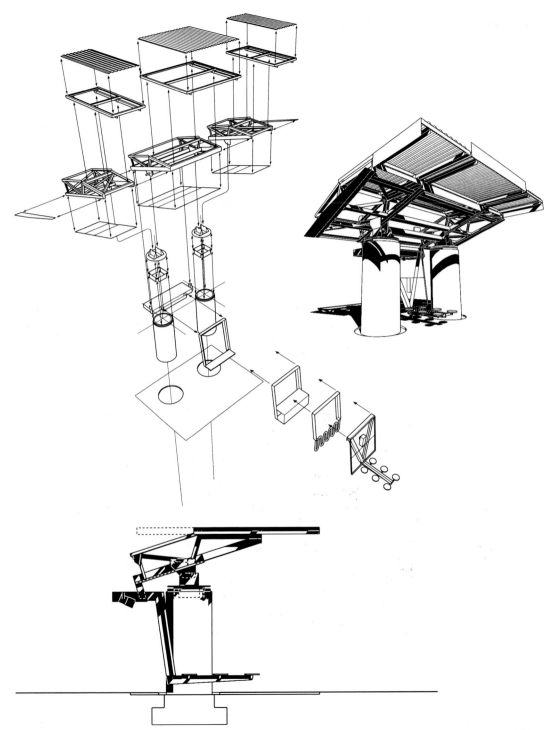

Roof like a liquid flung over the Plaza

2001-2003
Memphis, Tennessee,
Usa

This object with a powerful visual impact is made of steel with a mirror surface and looks like a solidified jet of liquid. It has an area of 445 square metres. The structure that supports the stainless-steel panels is thread-like and forms seats at the base of the columns. The smallest column, the one near the building, can hold from ten to twelve people and serve as a meeting room; the largest column provides up to thirty seats and can be used as an space for performances.

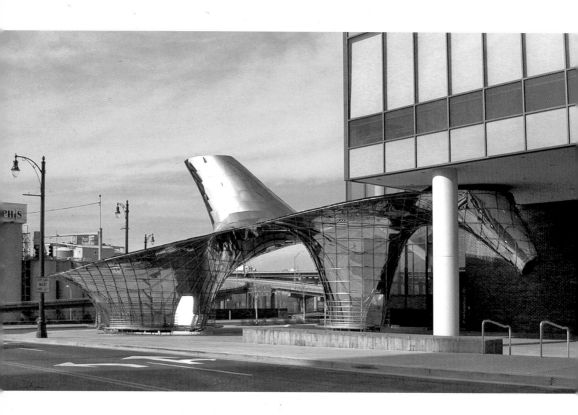

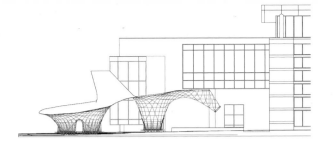

Richard Horden
T.U. Munich

Cliffhanger

1997
Lake Garda, Italy

This extreme shelter on the cliffs of Lake Garda is designed for surfers and climbers and to serve as an observation post for regattas. The elements that make up this architecture are few, lightweight and easy to transport and assemble: aluminium tubing for the structure and a sheet of reinforced fibre glass that is tied without particular difficulty to the structure itself. In this small shelter the technology used by sailors is combined with the one used by climbers.

Arata Isozaki

Loggia for the Uffizi Exit

1998
Florence, Italy

The project for upgrading the square is made up at ground level of a flat part and a sloping part. This makes it possible to connect the museum gradually with the city and at the same time provide the museum itself with a protected space in front of the exit. The external space is sheltered by a very sober loggia whose presence creates a small plaza. The loggia consists of a steel pergola faced with pietra serena and transparent parts in polycarbonate. The loggia houses a row of four statues, situated in line with the exits.

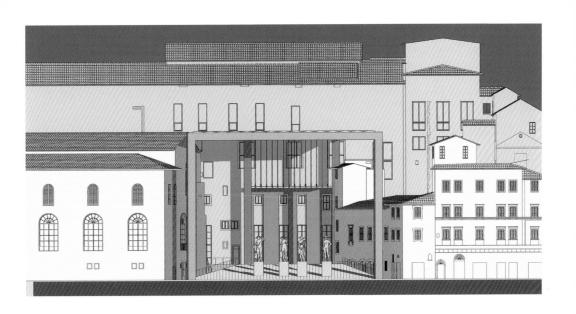

Terminus multimodal Hoenheim Nord

1999-2001
Strasbourg, France

The programme called for the creation of an interchange between private vehicular traffic and the trams that run to the city centre. This entailed the creation of an open-air car park with 700 places and a station covering 3000 m². The project is structured around the continual overlapping of fields and abstract lines that are connected together to form a dynamic whole. The fields transcribe the pattern of movement generated by the cars, trams, bicycles and pedestrians, each of which has its own trajectory and track. The station is built of concrete facing slabs supported by piers of galvanized steel.

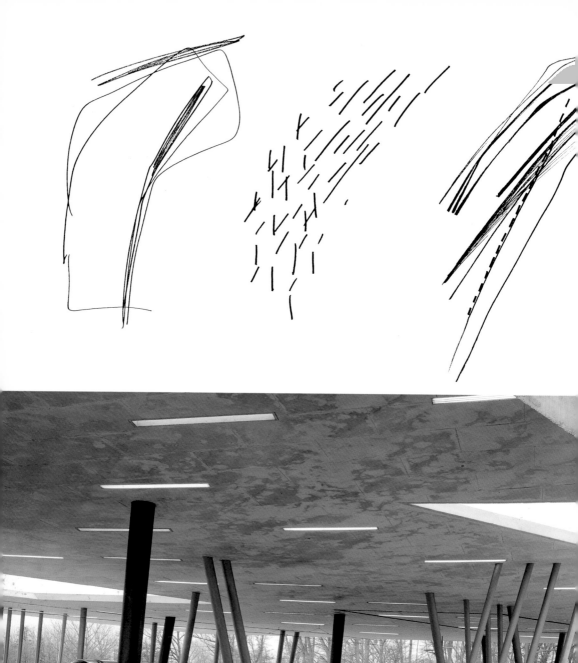

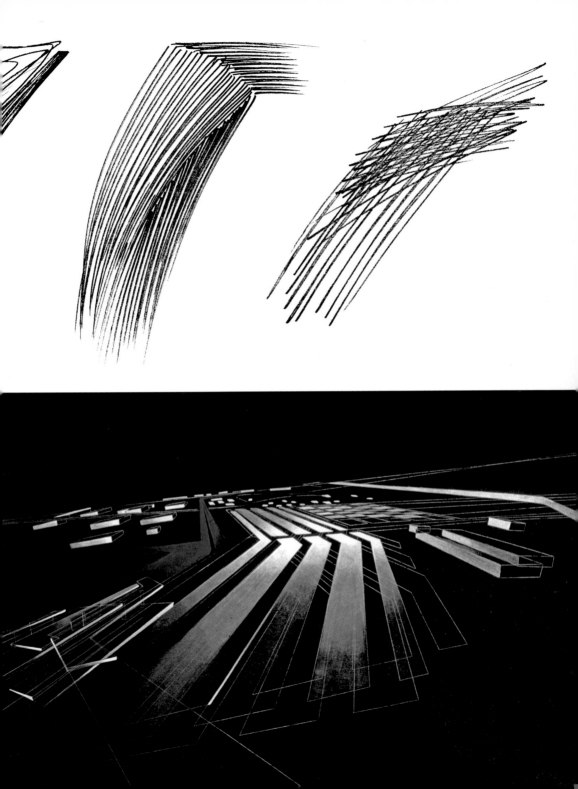

From volumes to holes
Kengo Kuma

I want to "erase" architecture. This is how I've always felt; this is how I will continue to feel. I became strongly aware of this feeling of wanting to make architecture disappear when I took on a project to build an observatory on Mt. Kiro on Oshima and stood at the spot where the building was to be erected. I was asked to design an observatory atop this small island in the Inland Sea that would serve as the symbol of the town. The summit had already been bulldozed flat and was being used as a park. Although the mountain offered a breathtaking view of the Inland Sea, the summit, which had been lopped off, was a sad sight. I felt very strongly that any building erected there should disappear, no matter what.

My building was the complete opposite of a monument to the city which the town mayor had had in mind. My plan was to restore the summit to its original shape and bury the observatory. I covered the ground with soil to recreate the original shape of the mountain, planted greenery, and gave back the mountain its original appearance. I then buried the building, with the final result looking like a slit bisecting the peak. As a result, the building did not appear as a foreign object that stood out from the surrounding environment, but rather, as a "hole" that had appeared in the environment. If architectural objects can be considered as "male" structures, then buried structures can be regarded as "female" architecture. Up to now, human beings have almost exclusively built "male" architecture. During times when resources were believed to be infinite, and when the environment was believed to have infinite capacity, people favored this "male" form of architecture. Now that we know how delicate and fragile the environment is, however, the value of "male" architecture is being questioned.

This project became a turning point for me. However, I cannot design all my buildings to be buried in the ground. There may be cases where burying buildings in soil would destroy the environment or entail too much extra energy or cost. For the Hiroshige Museum, I tried to blend the structure with the environment by breaking down the building into particles. The goal was to break down the solid, heavy mass of the building into light, delicate particles.

The important point here is the type of particles to choose. In the case of Hiroshige Museum, I chose small louvers made of cedar wood, grown on the mountain behind the museum. Locally grown materials blend easily with the natural environment without putting pressure on it. In the old days, Japanese carpenters used lumber felled in the mountains as close as possible to their workplace. The size of the particles is also important, since they should balance the size of the particles that comprise the surrounding environment. With the Hiroshige Museum, for example, I carefully studied the heights of the trees on the mountain behind the building and the diameters of their branches, and decided that, in terms of balance, the cross-sectional dimension of each wooden louver should be 3 mm x 6 mm. If the particles of the building were too large, they themselves would stand out and detract attention from the building itself; if they were too small, the particles would appear to blend back into a single mass, rendering their purpose ineffective.

The same techniques that were used in the Ukiyoe art of Hiroshige have been used in the design. He used overlapping particles to express three dimensions instead of large surfaces of color (see Fig. 1). The rain is first drawn as particles in this woodblock print, and a number of other spaces overlap in the background. Transparent layers are created with particles, and these layers overlap one another, expressing depth. Conversely, a technique called "perspective" is used to express three dimensions in Western paintings. With the perspective technique, objects that are far away are drawn smaller, and the comparison of small and large objects, and lines that radiate from the vanishing point combine to express depth. With this method, the space does not need to be transparent. Western painters in the twentieth century learned the concept of "transparency" from Hiroshige. Frank Lloyd Wright recognized the revolutionary aspects of Hiroshige's Ukiyoe art, and in addition to becoming a collector and purchasing many of his woodblock prints, he incorporated the transparency of Hiroshige's prints into his architecture. The "transparency" that is one of the fundamental principles of modernist architecture in the twentieth century and that was introduced to the world by Wright's architecture is an evolution of this transparency, and its roots can be traced back to Hiroshige's art.

Hiroshige's technique resembles "sfumato", a technique contrived by Leonardo da Vinci. Just as paint can be broken down into particles and blended, blurring the contour of a shape, the contour of a building, too, can be made to dissolve in an ambiguous fashion. The result is the environment and the building coming together and being melded into a single unit. However, although sfumato can blend and blur objects, it cannot give transparency to the object. During the process of making a wood block print, transparency is derived from the numerous layers of overlapping prints.

Another very interesting thing about this woodblock print (Fig. 1) are the extremely geometrical straight lines that are used to express rain, a natural element. There are not considered to be any artists that used straight lines to express rain in Europe before this Ukiyoe was created in the nineteenth century. There was a stark contrast between how natural and manmade objects were expressed, with straight lines often being used to express manmade objects, and almost never used to express things found in nature. However, there is no contrast between manmade objects and nature in Ukiyoe. In addition to the world of Ukiyoe, the same can be said about the world of music.

The contrast between natural and manmade objects is at the root of Western culture, and in fact, this contrast served as the driving force behind all Western culture. On the other hand, the spirit of bringing nature and manmade objects as close as possible to one another exists in Japanese culture. People tend to dislike harsh nature, and like a quiet, gentle refined version of nature that is not overpowering..

This can also be considered an extension of the "hole" technique I discovered at the Hiroshige Ando Museum and Kiro Observatory. The Mt. Kiro observatory comprises a large hole. Likewise, the space between one louver and another is a hole. Light filters through these holes, creates pleasant shadows, and allows the wind to pass through. These holes delicately connect people with the outside environment.

For many years, architecture was perceived as "volume." The rough, crude methods of calculation used in capitalist society focus constantly on volume and nothing else. However, what the human spirit and body really seek is not objects or volume, but holes.

Utagawa Hiroshige, *Sudden cloud-burst on the Great bridge near Atake*, 1857

Isamu Noguchi, Jefferson
Memorial Park, 1945

Environment

A series of non-volumetric elements located in a public space create an environment, i.e. a field formed by the dialogue between different objects. The concept is that of Isamu Noguchi's playground, something like a game played on an urban scale. This is how Noguchi himself describes the logic of his invention: '...empty space has no visual dimension or signification in itself. Scales and meaning appear, instead, only when an object or a line is introduced... the size and the shape of each element is entirely relative to all other elements and given space'. Thus the playground is a system of composition that, as often happens in non-volumetric architecture, is applied on different scales of intervention without changing its intrinsic logic.

In post-modernity the playground has come to be structured in a definitive manner, involving not just the public spaces but also the buildings. This success is due both to the technical ability of the playground to bond together interventions made up of fragments, and to the need to satisfy the taste for play typical of our age, which sees the public place as a place of recreation. The *non*-volumetric environment also presents different configurations from that of the playground, such as the individual object blown up to an urban or territorial scale which, owing to its enticing scenery, determines the character of a place. Sometimes the environment does not originate from planning in advance, but from the "happening" of self-construction. The difference of the two approaches is indicative of the ever more noticeable gap that has emerged between the world of design, which verges on aspects reminiscent of art nouveau, and that of participation, totally uninterested in pretensions to an *a priori* stylistic unity.

Wes Jones

The Golden plate

1997
San Francisco,
California, Usa

The project for Union Square in San Francisco sets out to make its own functions obvious. Thus the underground car park is not completely buried, but visible in a succession of views from the level of the city. The services on the other hand are located at various points of an exuberant steel structure that is set on the existing columns and positioned at a higher level than that of the street. This level is accessible from the city by a series of ramps, staircases and footbridges which offer unexpected views of the structure beneath. Overall, the project presents a strong image that magnifies the way it functions and renders it spectacular. This is based on the hypothesis that contemporary urban design cannot be confined to the mere plastic definition of the architecture.

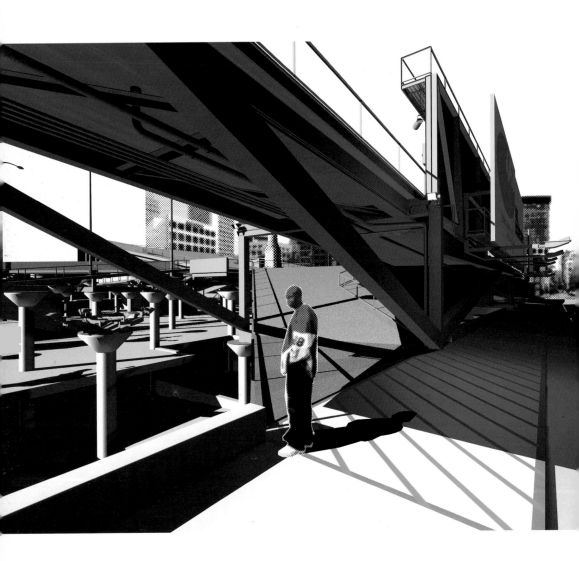

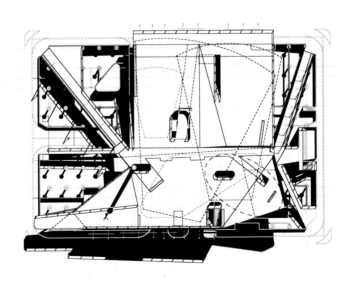

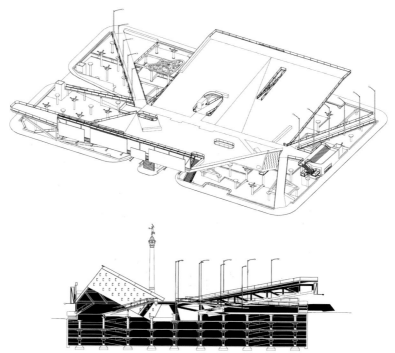

Italo Rota
and partners

Underpass in Misano

1997-1999
Misano, Italy

The station and underpass of Misano are located in the vicinity of the town centre. The underpass serves to create a continuity between the two zones of the city, the one facing the sea and the one located higher up, and takes the form of a natural continuation of the street above, which is also the city's main road, where people are accustomed to take a stroll. Above the underpass is situated the railway station, which is a simple canopy supported by a series of full-height columns that protects the easy climb. The project is clearly laid out and in scale with its context; this clarity is enhanced by a decorative system of colours and lights, designed specially for a seaside resort whose principal source of income is tourism.

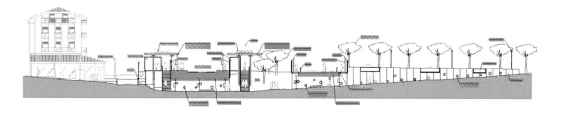

Vlotho Fortress

1998-2003
Vlotho, Ost-Westfalen,
Germany

The ruins of a medieval castle that dominates the city of Vlotho have been subjected to an intervention carried out by the LOMA group with the aim of bringing back to life a tourist attraction that has long been in a state of decay. The idea was to combine the restoration of the castle proper with new dot-like interventions, of which the most conspicious is a 50-metre-high transmission tower for a local radio. The central element of the project is a platform called the 'stone parquet'. A route leads from the platform to a panoramic balcony projecting from the walls. Where the masonry was badly damaged, the walls have been repaired by means of gabions containing stones of a different colour. In general LOMA has sought to avoid any mimicry of the pre-existent structure, but at the same time to utilize neutral forms and materials, which do not enter into competition with the location.

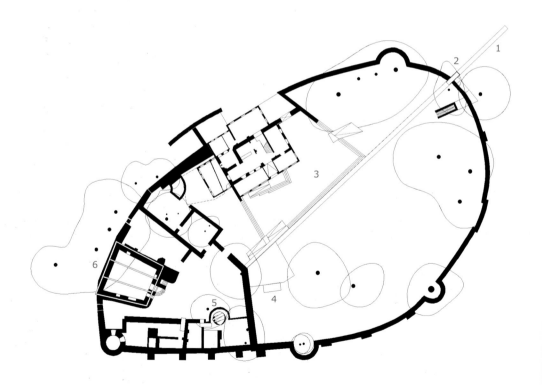

north

east

west

south

1989

2002-2006
Barcelona, Spain

The Gran Via de les Corts Catalanes in Barcelona consists in the redesign of a road section in such a way as to divide it into several different levels. The aim is to create a double linear park on the upper level, at the sides of the carriageways. To achieve this one part of the upper roadway juts out over the level below. Thus the philosophy behind the intervention is to consider the design of infrastructures no longer as a transcription of simple traffic requirements, but as an opportunity to rewrite structured and multifunctional pieces of city. The planners have also devoted their attention to other aspects of the project, right down to the scale of street furniture.

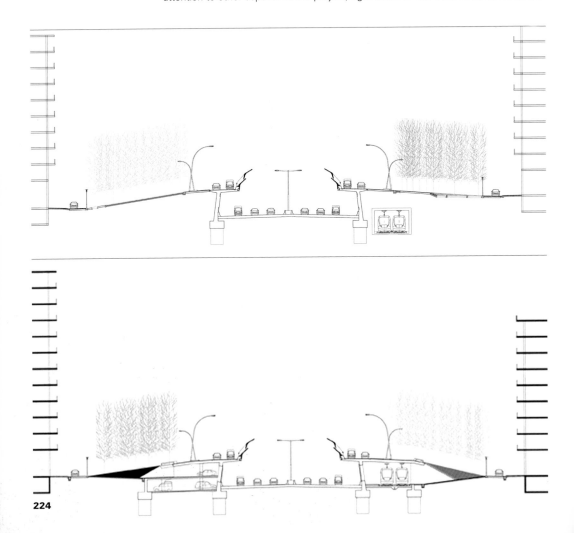

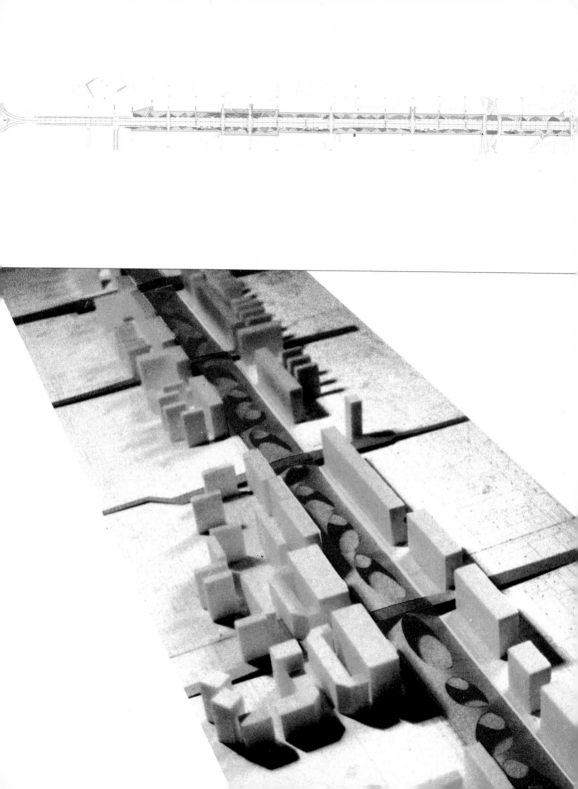

High botanic bridge

2001-2002
Gwangju, South Korea

At Gwangju the West 8 studio was asked to find a solution for 11 kilometres of disused railway passing near the city centre. The idea it came up with was that of the 'green serpent', i.e. a linear park connecting up 20 schools that face onto the disused railway line. The salient feature of the promenade is a bridge decorated with a sequence of 24 concrete vases holding the most important species of tree in South Korea. Given its dimension and its visual impact (the structure rises 35 m above the ground), the botanic bridge conceived by West 8 is intended as a 'euphoric landmark', a symbol of the attention to cultivated nature characteristic of the Korean tradition.

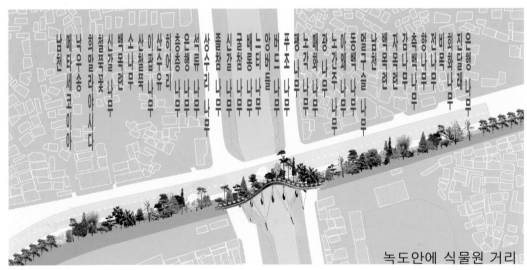

녹도안에 식물원 거리

광주천을 넘어가는 식물원

광주의 새로운 푸른길

식물원속의 다리

보행로에서 바라본 풍경

옆에서 본 다리

1999-2001
Malacca, Malaysia

The intervention is located inside a lot measuring sixty by six metres that used to contain an ornate building which has now almost completely vanished. The idea is to leave everything in a ruined state, while introducing four small volumes housing services into the lot, now a garden. The dominant presence is that of the small courtyards which are created through the introduction of the volumes. As a whole, these produce the appearance of a timeless and fascinating scene of dereliction. The environmentally friendly vein of the intervention is underlined by the use of salvaged materials that have been given new functions, such as a fallen wooden beam turned into a bench or the granite thresholds that have become elements of the outdoor paving.

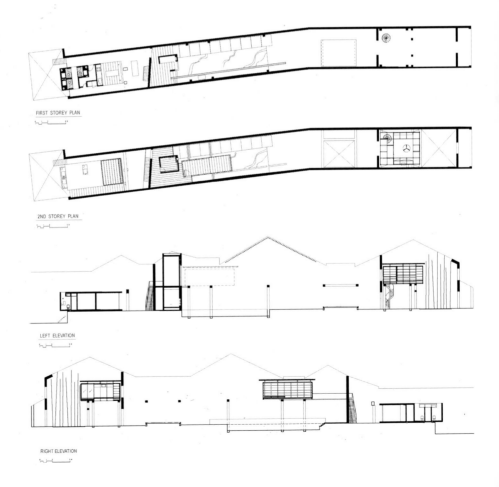

FIRST STOREY PLAN

2ND STOREY PLAN

LEFT ELEVATION

RIGHT ELEVATION

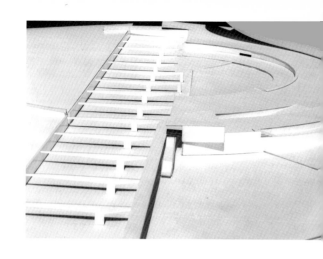

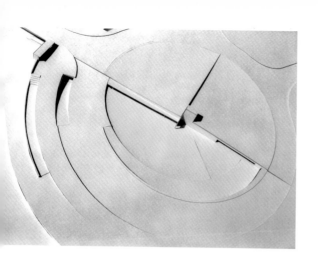

1998-2002
Palma de Mallorca,
Baleari Islands, Spain

The intervention is set in a key zone of Palma de Mallorca and its dimension is such as to make it an important public place. The choice was to subdivide the ground level with a series of earth movements that would create different settings with different atmospheres, as well as making it possible to isolate them from the surrounding scenery. The memory of how the area used to be is entrusted to the trace of a railway line that has served as a cue for the overall configuration of the project. The park, with its movements of earth and thematic stations, finds its antecedent in Isamu Noguchi's playground.

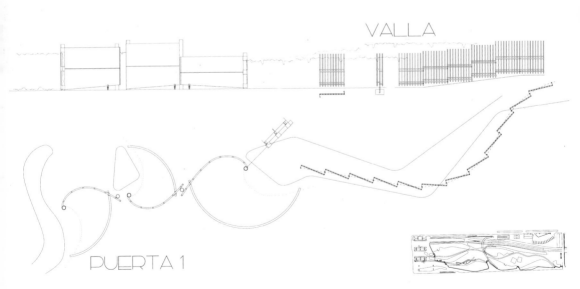

VALLA

PUERTA 1

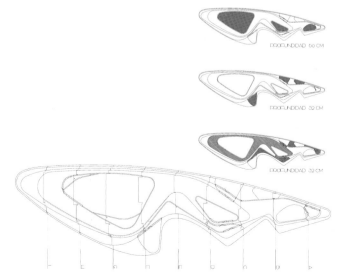

PROFUNDIDAD 60 CM

PROFUNDIDAD 32 CM

PROFUNDIDAD 32 CM

MONTICULOS

CAMINOS

VEGETACION

O   PAVIMENTO

236

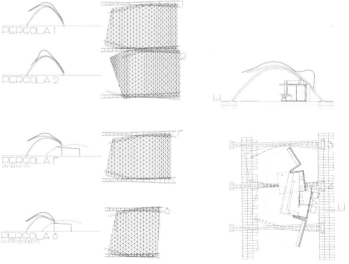

Ciudad abierta

1969-...
Valparaíso, Cile

A group of about thirty people decided to create their own environment. It was all about a change of life, not of world. In 1969 they bought a levelled area of land by the Pacific and formed a cooperative, which they called Amereida (America + Eneida [Aeneid]) and decided to create a 'town' using their own resources. It was interpreted as an incessant 'return to unknowing', advancing in the construction of the work using cheap, affordable elements, such as tree trunks, bricks and slabs, although this did not limit the spatial and technical innovations. So the idea of the Cooperativa Amereida is that no such thing as a previously defined project for a town exists, just a humble and everyday working in the field, the only way to ensure the architecture is transformed into landscape.

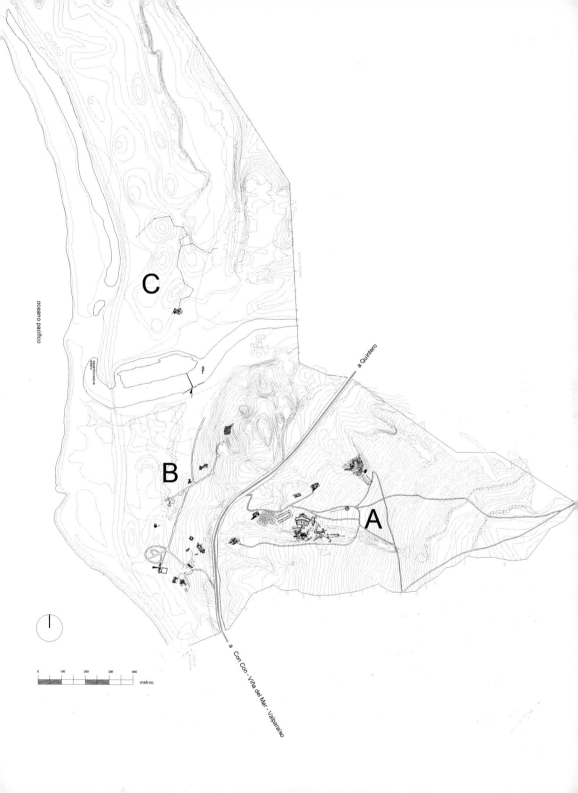

oceano pacifico

C

B

A

a Quintero

a Con Con - Viña del Mar - Valparaiso

0   100   200   300   400

metros

in this way, the works combine lightness with the original availability of the location, such as to determine interior spaces founded on themselves and on the natural environment that surrounds them.

Thus we built the works of the Ciudad abierta and also those of the Crossings. These works give life to an inside space lived in the open air, in a natural environment in which the architecture acquires the dimension of lightness and availability; all of this through a lived architectural experience. A type of experience that combines the lightness of poetry, of what comes from within, with the availability of nature, which is found outside.

This is our interpretation of un-volumetric architecture in the Ciudad abierta.

The Crossings

We set off for the Paraná to gather working elements for the Architectural Workshop on the access road to Valparaíso, as an urban value that directs residential development towards an experience of what the place is.

For that reason, we went to visit the riverside towns. We went to see a large river highway for the continent and everything it has generated on its boundaries. Before this we had been to Amazonia, to Iquitos.

During the 10-day Crossing we saw an ocean of fresh water that flowed down from north to south along the Paraguay–Paraná river system, and advanced with a current of visible water, capable of slowing down the progress of the boats travelling against the current. We learnt that this dynamic living water flows at a gradient of 1:10.000, which means that in 1 meter it falls 1/10 of a millimetre.

We also learnt that, in order to protect themselves from the flooding of the river, which can reach up to 7m in height - not due to tides, as in the ocean, but caused by the violent storms and the slow flow of the waters - some towns have built earth dikes at the boundary between the inhabited area and the river, in order to avoid being flooded by the rising waters.

From the Amereida workshop we received "The Poem of the Phalene" for us to take with us and share during the Crossing.

How could we do it?

Words need a medium to be written on. So we thought of a layer of plaster on which to print the words, or some tiers capable of building an embankment with a stairway. The poem could thus be split into 10 parts, so into 10 tiers. 10 tiers measuring 70 x 35 x 7 cm = 411 kg, equivalent to the weight of 6 people, to take on the bus.

We had a week to make the tiers in Valparaíso, before leaving. After passing through Paraná, Santa Elena, Esquina, Goya, Empedrado, Corrientes, Formosa, Asunción, we arrived in Concepción.

"Here!" – we said. And we went to explore the river's edge.

We found two possible places, a wall along the embankment and a stairway, and we chose the stairway. Vertical or horizontal? We decided to arrange them horizontally, every two tiers. So we built a stairway in the stairway, descending from the dike to the river.

In Concepción, for those who pass by and sit on the steps looking at the river, the verses of the poem, seen with the corner of the eye and deposited in the memory, make up a new way of looking at the river in the presence of poetry.

In the Amazon River we placed a fragment of the poem Amereida, written on glossy paper, inside some sealed floating objects, which we then threw into the river for the current to take them... to all the towns downriver.

So we studied the sign, as the opposite value to the architectural work, which represents steadiness and stability. But the opposite, if understood as "absence", reveals poetically the reality of its own lightness.

On both rivers, the work was therefore none other than a surface on which to write a poem, a greeting from the architects to the inhabitants of the river. Because the river does not accept light works on its banks, so on the Paraná the poem is on a work already existing, the steps, while on the Amazon... it floats.

Crossing between Two Continental Banks
Our crossing had two orientations.
The first, that conceived in the Architectural Workshop, takes up the continental dimension to study the boundaries of Valparaíso, enclosed between the Andes mountain range above and the Pacific Ocean below. The second is dedicated to the Crossing work by Godofredo Iommi.

Coperativa Amereida,
Ciudad abierta, partial plan

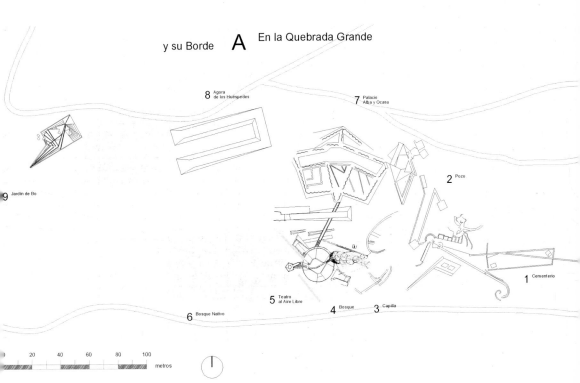

y su Borde **A** En la Quebrada Grande

8 Agora de los Huéspedes

7 Palacio Alba y Ocaso

9 Jardín de Bo

2 Pozo

1 Cementerio

5 Teatro al Aire Libre

4 Bosque

3 Capilla

6 Bosque Nativo

20 40 60 80 100 metros

During a class in the Amereida Workshop, we were read a text by God-ofredo Iommi from 1994, "Ah, atravesada Phalene".

We reread it several times and from it we extracted the following passage:
"¿qué haremos? ¿en la travesía atravesante?

Y se hacen los signos ¿cuáles? Los que van a decirle a la tierra, con-struida, descampada o no, que es lo que indica la Musa para que siguien-do su curso se dé curso al destino Americano de Amereida en ese allí, así".

("What will we do? In the crossing crossing?

And signs are made. Which? Those that will tell the earth, built on, open or not, what the Muse indicates so that, following her course, it will be possi-ble to deal with the American destination of Amereida down there, that way".)

So we decided to attach a sign, made of a seat and a belvedere. To con-template, sitting or leaning, and read in the territory what the Muse indi-cates; thus living the highest form of artistic contemplation, with eyes framed in the 5 orientations of the cube from a three-dimensional window with a 1.40m side, painted blue, which here is the colour of lightness.

On one of its sides we placed a plaque that reads:

"To the poet Godofredo Iommi, School of Architecture, Catholic Uni-versity of Valparaíso, Crossing of October 2001".

We conceived our dedication to Godo as "a greeting", thinking of the work as "an architectural sign", a primary expression.

In that location, this small blue cube made of void acquired an order-ing grandeur:

everything converged towards it, and from it arose the axis that from the main ravine lead to the Pacific, and to the two side ravines, which thus form a triangulation at the vertex of which we placed this sign, which, at dusk, when we left, we saw shining immersed in the darkness of the hills.

All this was seen with a continental eye, an eye that had made many Crossings of America and that sees grandeur and power in the dimensions of the location; yet these features cannot be considered in isolation, but appear through the manifestation of a lightness and an original positivity.

As has already been said, "both experiences, that of the Ciudad abier-ta and that of the Crossings, are born from hearing the poetic word of Amereida" and "this has enabled us to understand that the relationship with the earth must be light".

We observe this relationship between the poetic word and lightness, for example, in the greeting, in the gesture and in the title of the paint-ing: "Bonjour Monsieur Courbet". It is an ascetic act. Precise, neither a gesture too little nor or a word too much.

Thus a greeting to the vastness of the poem of Amereida becomes one of the moments of American creativity and does so showing also "the des-tination of the work in relation to its natural location, discovering and pro-claiming the positivity of lightness". We see all this in the small dimen-sions of the work and in the blue of the cube, in the immensity of the An-des mountain range and in the fragility of the tiers and the objects float-ing in the powerful currents of American rivers.

To the lightness of what is small and fragile and to the positivity of the triangulation in the Andean ravine and the rising rivers we must add another dimension: briefness. Because the works of Crossing are conceived, designed and built in a brief time, a limited time, always initial, not fixed but fleeting: the time of travelling around America.

We think that these Crossing works, as well as conserving the poetic aspect of the American destiny of Amereida, contribute to defining the Un-Volumetric, to open up a new field of study in this way together with you.

For that reason, this text is not intended to limit itself to being either an essay or a report, but proposes to contribute to defining a new "architectural" value, it too light and brief.

This is our interpretation of Un-Volumetric architecture in America.

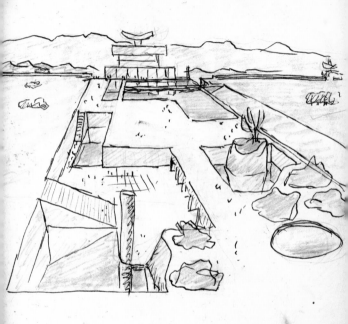

12 avril (2)
52

Earthworks

In the contemporary world there is an ever greater attraction to the ground, which has led in its most radical forms to an attempt to amalgamate the building with the land on which it stands. The influence of works of Land Art is undeniable here, and even today they continue to offer a fascinating catalogue of the ways in which earthworks can produce configurations of a clearly architectural character. Over the last decade earthworks have become one of the principal features of public space. This is primarily due to reasons of a technical character, in that they make it possible to characterize an environment using only a few means. To this is added the fact that they represent one of the most effective expressions of a more general trend to put natural materials on a par with artificial ones, and increasingly to favour the former. It should also be noted that the configurations and shapes typical of earthworks possess an intrinsic capacity for communication, as if they were able to give rise to an alternative world, made up archaic gestures and primary symbols. So we have gone well beyond the historic symbolism of the tumulus or the modernist architectural handling of the ground, which can be seen for example in the plateau of Chandigarh. Today cuts in the ground, reliefs and geometric working of the land, in most cases along fluid and rhythmic lines, reflect the growing tendency to enrich architecture with something that transcends it, that raises it to the level of a symbolic story with mass-appeal.

Ricardo Bofill

Volcans d'Auvergne Service area

1990-1991
Clermont Ferrand,
France

The character of this intervention derives from the nature of the site, a volcanic region of intense colours and extraordinary light. A sequence of circular spaces has been designed in consonance with the forms of the nearby area of Les Puys, characterized by a large number of craters. They are ringed on their perimeter by dunes that create a visual and acoustic barrier protecting them from the Autoroute. The parking and rest area covers 39.7 ha and comprises a filling station, cafeteria, restaurant, hotel and facilities for people making a stopover.

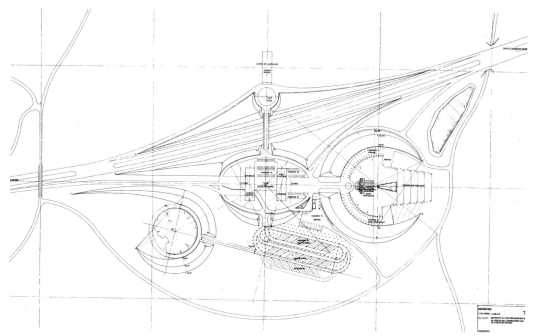

Grande Cretto at Gibellina

1985-1989
Gibellina, Italy

In 1968 a violent earthquake struck the town of Gibellina, destroying it completely. Faced with the impossibility of rebuilding the town, the decision was taken to leave a monument to its memory on the site. The task was entrusted to Alberto Burri, who between 1985 and 1989 created the *Great Crack*, a gigantic version of the artist's famous *Cracks*, pictures with fissured and fractured monochrome surfaces.

The work takes the form of an enormous blanket of white concrete measuring 300 by 400 m and traversed by crevices marking the position of what had once been Gibellina's streets. The ruins of the old buildings were cut off at a height varying from 1.50 to 2.00 metres and filled with their own rubble. Finally the whole thing was rendered uniform with a layer of white concrete. Thus the *Great Crack* is like a white shroud covering what is left of the town, and at the same time evokes the earth that shakes and kills.

Carlos Ferrater
Xavier Martí

West beach promenade in Benidorm

2002-2003
Benidorm, Spain

The promenade of Benidorm is intended to provide a new space of transition between the city and the sea. The project redesigns a new sinuous and organic topography, evocative of the rocks, the waves and the movements of the tide. The new landscape also redesigns the descents to the sea from the car parks and rest areas. The promenade consists of a series of overlapping layers: the first is that of the perimeter, made of white concrete, the second that of the areas paved in different materials and colours, the third that of the facilities and the last one that of the new plantings of trees and the water.

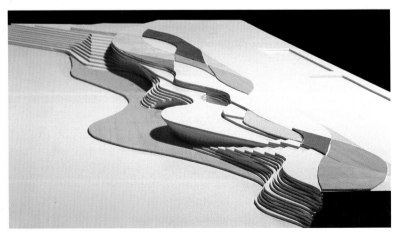

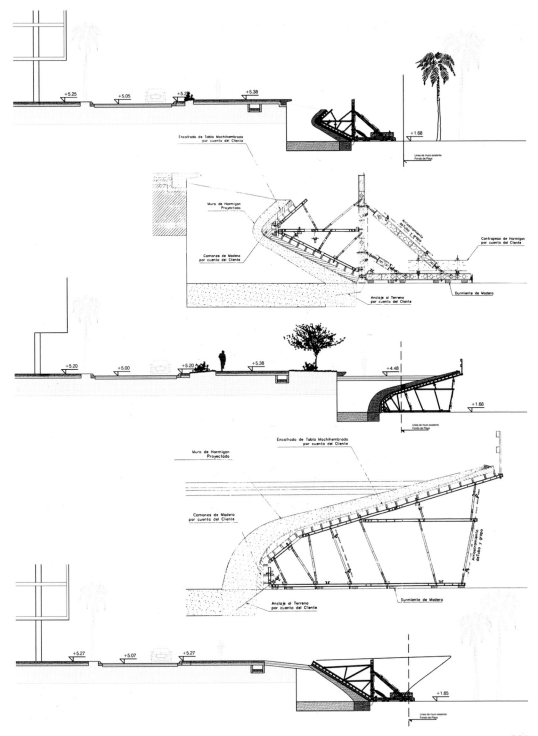

Encofrado de Tabla Machihembrada
por cuenta del Cliente

Muro de Hormigon
Proyectado

Comones de Madera
por cuenta del Cliente

Arriostramiento
de tubo y grapa

Contrapeso de Hormigon
por cuenta del Cliente

Anclaje al Terreno
por cuenta del Cliente

Durmiente de Madera

+5.25   +5.05   +5.28   +5.38   +1.68

Linea de muro existente
Fondo de Playa

+5.20   +5.00   +5.20   +5.38   +4.48   +1.68

Linea de muro existente
Fondo de Playa

Muro de Hormigon
Proyectado

Encofrado de Tabla Machihembrada
por cuenta del Cliente

Comones de Madera
por cuenta del Cliente

Arriostramiento
de tubo y grapa

Anclaje al Terreno
por cuenta del Cliente

Durmiente de Madera

+5.27   +5.07   +5.27   +1.65

Linea de muro existente
Fondo de Playa

261

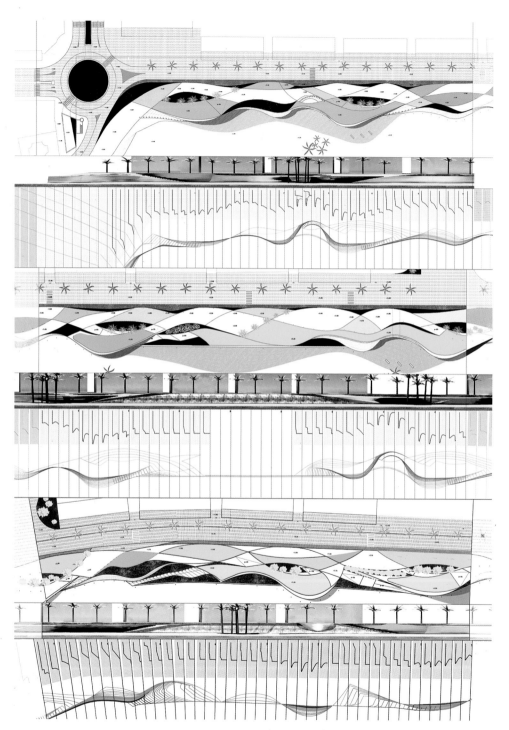

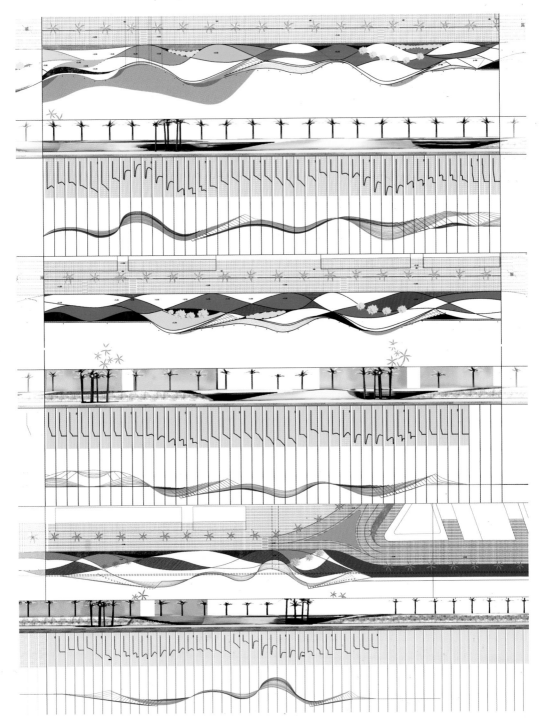

Atelier Marc Barani

Extension of the cemetery Saint-Pancrace

1990-1992
Roquebrune
Cap-Martin, France

The cemetery has been extended by making deep excavations in the hillside, contained by walls that protrude from the steep ridge. The excavations contain a monochromatic world of white stone and concrete that faces onto the sea below in a succession of terraces. The atmosphere is one of metaphysical calm, and is intended to inspire meditation and reconciliation with life through the view of the sea and nature.

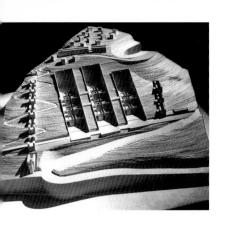
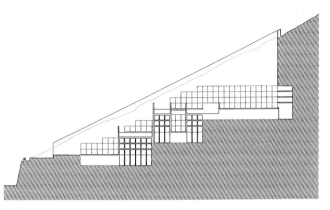

Lucien Den Arend

Homage to El Lissitzki

1985-1986
Lelystad, Netherlads

Homage to El Lissitzki is an earthwork located on the test circuit of the Dutch transport centre, an area reclaimed from the sea and drained. The designer was able to make use of 17,000 cubic metres of leftover earth to create this crescent, whose summit rises to the maximum height permitted by the amount of earth available. The idea of the project is taken from Land Art, the concept of a simple geometric figure identifying a place.

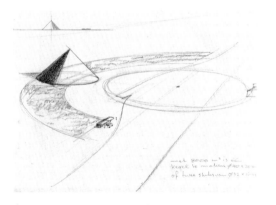

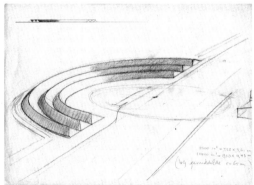

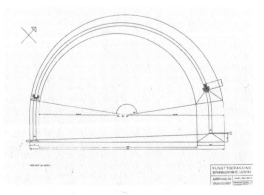

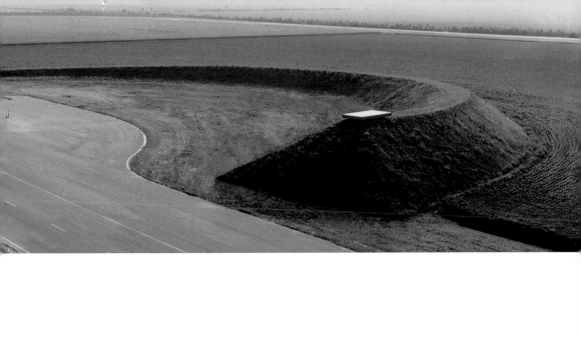

Arnaldo Pomodoro

Design for the New Cemetery of Urbino

1978
Urbino, Italy

The project proposes the incisions characteristic of Arnaldo Pomodoro's sculpture on a territorial scale, adapting the artist's unmistakable style to the needs of a cemetery. A perfectly circular hill is cut through by a path, onto which face the tombs. Transverse arms radiate outwards from the main route, and are also cut into the perfect natural geometry. The hilly mound has no vegetation, but is protected at the base by an unbroken ring of trees.

Design for the New Cemetery of Urbino

1978
Urbino, Italy

The project alludes to such archetypal and historical figures as the stepped pyramid, the Tower of Babel and the tumulus, but also contains references to natural craters and cultivated terraces. The great earthwork proposed by Superstudio is composed of a series of terraces with a ring of cypresses at the top that project this architecture of earth towards the sky. Superstudio's project can to all intents and purposes be considered a perfect fusion of its own brand of radical architecture and the citational tendencies of the early post-modern.

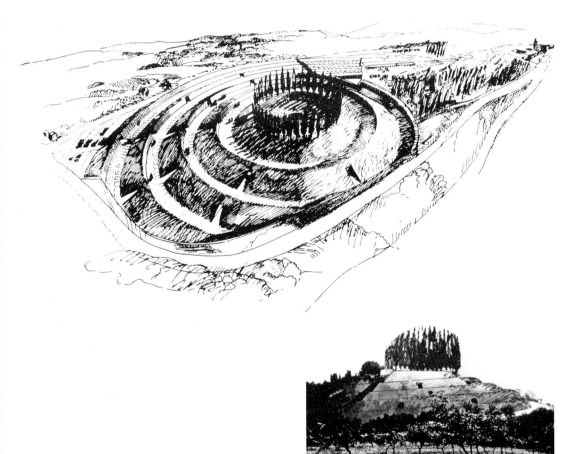

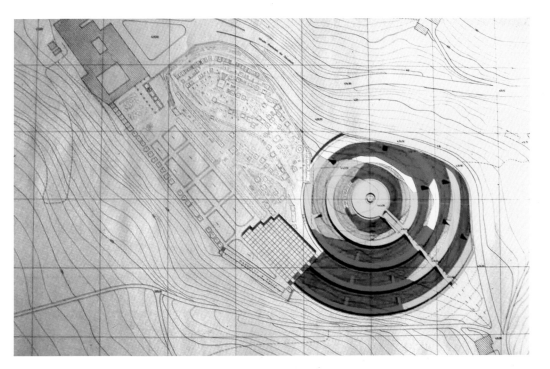

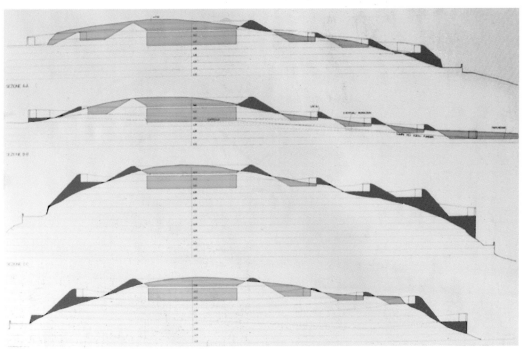

Wes Jones   **Lifeguard Tower**

1988   This design for a lifeguard tower could be considered an illustration of Heidegger's
Venice Beach,   claim that 'technology teases nature into unhiddenness'. The job of the typical
California, Usa   lifeguard tower is to provide the lifeguards with a vantage point from which they
                             can keep an eye on the swimmers they protect. This project supplies the lifeguards
                             with the simplest version of this requirement: a dune. No dune may actually be
                             present on the beach, so a machine is brought in to construct one, demonstrating
                             the effort requited to achieve a 'natural' condition.

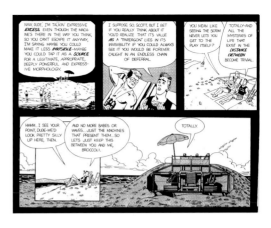

Hannu Siren   **Responsibility**

1992-1995
Otawiemi, Finland

The town council called in the author after realizing that the work of excavation on which it had embarked to widen the road was compromising the appearance of the place. Siren then directed the work of excavation in such a way as to turn an intrusive intervention into an opportunity for landscaping. To exercise better control over the work the artist made a series of models in clay. The intervention extends for a length of 200 m and reaches 7 m in the highest part. At night the intervention of artistic excavation is enhanced by a spectacular lighting system.

Onl Oosterhuis
Lénárd

Parascape

1998
Kop Van Zuid,
Rotterdam,
Netherlands

Parascape is a sculpture/event whose aim is to interact with the public, influencing
its behaviour. Parascape is set on a flight of steps like a parasitic object, something
organic and soft, verging on the surreal. Ultimately, the idea is to create metaphorical
objects whose evocative power is able to entertain the public and thus create
a public place. In this case sculpture, architecture and design contribute in equal
measure to this end.

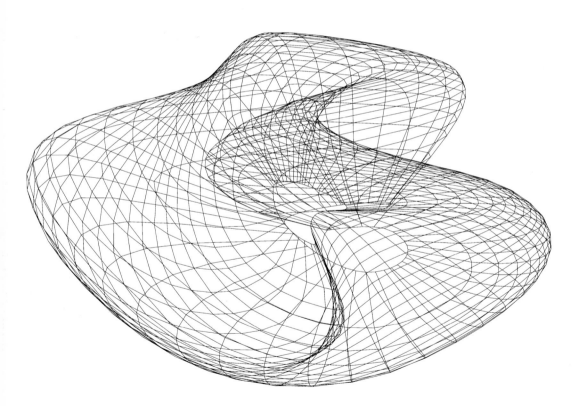

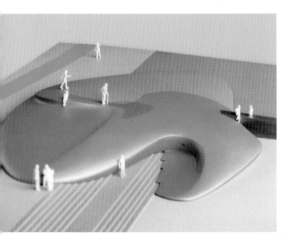

Protection Structures against snow avalanches in Iceland

1998-1999
Siglufjördur, Iceland

In 1995, following a series of avalanches, a national programme was launched in Iceland to forestall the damage caused by these events. The Landslag group contributed to this programme with the realization of two systems of defence for the small town of Siglufjördhur. They consist of two embankments that run above the town, one stretching for 700 m and the other for 200 m. The shape and height of the embankments have been designed in such a way as to reconcile technical requirements with those of a suitable insertion in the landscape.

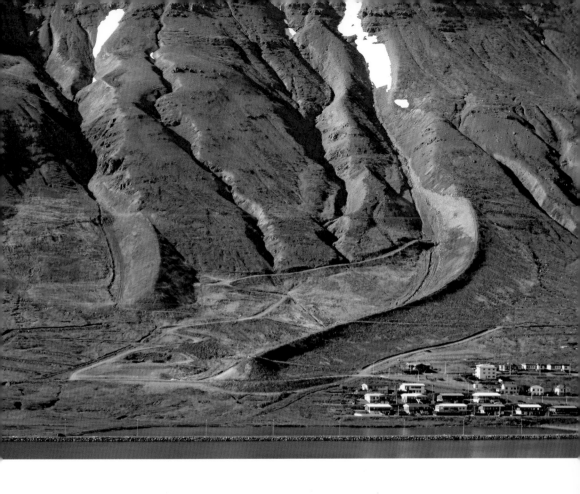

0 50 100 150 200

Peter Noever   **The Pit in the Breitenbrunn**

1971-1994
Breitenbrunn, Austria

This project called 'the pit' is an example of underground architecture that owes
a great deal to contemporary works of Land Art. A long cut in the ground is traversed
by another cut and finally encounters a circular excavation with a section in the
form of a truncated cone. The layout is hieratic in its simplicity and the figures
it creates in the landscape assume a symbolic significance. _function?_

Kengo Kuma

Kiro-san observatory

1994
Ehime, Japan

"I was asked to design an observatory atop this small island in the Inland Sea that would serve as the symbol of the town. The summit had already been bulldozed flat and was being used as a park. Although the mountain offered a breathtaking view of the Inland Sea, the summit, which had been lopped off, was a sad sight. I felt very strongly that any building erected there should disappear, no matter what" (Kengo Kuma).

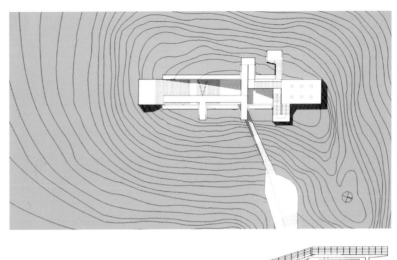

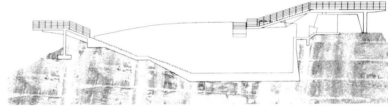

Land Design 2
Bernardo Secchi

About twenty years ago, in 1986, I wrote an article for *Casabella* entitled
'Progetto di suolo' ('Land Design'), a term that has since become very common in the language of architects and town planners. In those notes I argued that town planning is above all land design, that a considerable part
of the reflection on architecture has always been incorporated in land design and that the neglect of land design in the second half of the 20th century is one of the main causes of the semantic poverty of the contemporary city: a poverty that has resulted in increasingly reductive modes of
use of urban space and the territory and that has made the consolidated
city less and less attractive with respect to other forms of settlement, such
as the ones represented by the scattered city.

In those years I was engaged in the study and drafting of the Plan of
Siena and many of my reflections arose out of what has been for me 'the
lesson of Siena', i.e. from the experience of the medieval space that I was
creating in that city. Since that time I have had an opportunity to learn
other lessons from other cities.

Siena has always caught the imagination: not just of individuals, but also and above all the collective one. Anyone who has devoted time and attention to the city, its inhabitants and their history cannot help but notice
the force with which a whole sheaf of images has been deposited on the
city and has lasted over time. Like the other ancient cities of Europe, Siena
is part of the historical consciousness of a huge part of our world. The 20th
century has always planned the city with one eye on that of the past, in-
terpreting its principal lessons in a banal or sophisticated way. At the end
of the century that ancient city, Siena, provided some of those lessons.

The first level of reflections concerns the comfort of public space: a
question that is related not just to the forms, dimensions and articulation
of such spaces, but also to the conditions of the microclimate created by
the size of the areas that are not built on, by the orientation of the buildings around them and by the materials utilized for both. Siena's Piazza
del Campo, for instance: many important things have been said and written about this famous square, onto which face buildings dating from five
different centuries, about its form and the way in which it has been constructed. But most people's experience of the square has little to do with
all that. Anyone who has spent time observing the square, watching the
movement of sunlight and shade in different seasons and the effect this
has on which parts of it are frequented; anyone who has tried sitting on
the paving of this square, sheltered from the wind, and appreciated the
gentle warmth of the bricks and its slope; anyone who has noticed the simple ways in which the design of the paving facilitates the run-off of water

from this immense surface on rainy days, the ways in which the same design suggests the uses to which it should be put without imposing them, cannot help but agree that it is above all the great comfort of this public space that shapes people's experience of it and makes them appreciate it. We find the same sensation of well-being in Utrecht, in the less touristy parts of Venice or Amsterdam, cities that are not located on the margins of the contemporary urban experience, but at their centre.

The second level of reflections concerns the nature of the open space: of the streets, squares, courtyards and gardens, of the expanses of countryside that are enclosed, in Siena, by the city walls. What is so astonishing and bewildering about many European cities of the 20th century is the absence of such a significant and systematic experience of open space. Enormously expanded, the city seems to have been broken up into an episodic set of fragments connected together by spaces lacking a clear status. The open space of Siena, on the other hand, like that of many other medieval cities in Europe, has three principal and unambiguous statuses (Hunt, 1996; Secchi, 2000; Choay, 2003). To each of these, with their numerous variants, correspond different materials, designs and spatial experiences. The first is that of the public, the space where people find themselves in public and in which the main rituals of social life are performed, from festivals to the market, from processions to the 'stroll'. Collective and indefinite space, subject to the most varied interpretations and practices, the space of the public is an interior of the city constricted between the walls of the extremely closely packed buildings that face onto it. With sudden and significant leaps in scale, it expands into squares and other open spaces, enters the church as in the Nolli plan of Rome, creeps under the town hall and under the canopies of the market or warehouse, wedges itself into buildings through the twilight of the entrance hall, the portico or other specific places of mediation and opens up to a view of the surrounding countryside. Proust has left us a splendid description of the relations between the pressure exerted by the narrow space of the Venetian *calli* and by their succession and the sudden dilation of the *campo* or of the view of the basin and lagoon. Arriving at Piazza del Campo in Siena you undergo a similar spatial experience. A space that is interconnected but continually changing, the open space of the mediaeval city uses specific measures to establish relationships of great variety and complexity with the building. In its design, dictated by a fundamental economy of means of expression, we can recognize a constant attention to the solution of particular technical problems: how to make sure that water flows in the right way, how to use an imperceptible difference in level, how to utilize suitable materials. The Sienese aesthetic, like that of Bruges, Ascoli Piceno or many other places in Europe that have pride of place in the collective imagination as examples of the medieval city *par excellence*, does not depend just or so much on marvellous works of architecture, but on the way that these aspects are handled with a highly sophisticated minimalism. The second is the large and nearby open space of the countryside, the lagoon, the hills: of what lies outside the city and is different from it, which is a space to be looked at, walked in and used for produc-

Aereal view of the centre
of Siena

tion rather than for collective practices and rituals. Between these two experiences are situated, in the medieval city, the more intimate ones of courtyards, cloisters and numerous gardens partially concealed from view where the relations between people and activities can find expression in an endless series of gradations. The third status is that of secluded spaces, of the most absolute privacy and silence: spaces used for work and leisure, but also for communal life.

I have proposed the example of Siena in order to point out that land design does not concern public space alone, and still less is it confined to green areas: parks, gardens and playgrounds; that land design is not in opposition to the architectural object and not even a complement to it; that land design, finally, operates in three dimensions even if it does not necessarily imply the construction of volumes.

In recent years, significant projects of land design have been proposed all over Europe, and some of them are documented in this volume. But there have also been projects devoid of interest that have given it a reductive interpretation, that have brought it down to the mere solution of technical problems, however important, such as those connected with the road system and parking, or, even worse, to a question of street furniture.

There are two essentially complementary ways of approaching land design simply; at least they are the ones that I take. The first is to scan the topography of the territory, seeking to grasp its particular connotations, the things that make it specific and perhaps different, even if only slightly, from other territories, and then try to bring these out through an act of design. In the case of Kortrijk Cemetery, for example, we wanted to show that the region of Western Flanders, notwithstanding its mythical reputation as the *plat pays*, is not flat at all. A series of waves, like those of a solidified sea, run across it in regular fashion: long and gentle waves, with a length of a kilometre and a height of fifty meters. But these are precisely the measurements that interest us, measurements that modify the perception of the territory, the breadth of the horizons, depending on whether one is on the crest or in the trough of the wave. The cemetery, conceived as a route running from the crest down the slope of the wave, sets out to reveal this character of the territory, and for this reason has need of no more than a few, minimal signs.

The second is the one that interprets the territory, the land, as a stable support on which are set, embedded or simply inserted objects that are often less permanent, i.e. endowed with less inertia. Paola Viganò would call this architecture h=1 (Viganò, 1999). Mies's ITT Campus is an example. The ground becomes a bas-relief, an artificially constructed topography, with greater or lesser attention paid to the original characteristics of the territory, which is able to give new meaning to the space in between the buildings and, in this case, the campus as a whole. A theme that has become particularly relevant now that all of urban space is organized as if it were on a campus: objects freely arranged in a vast space. For a long time, ever since its origins at Princeton in the 18th century, the campus has been the location of the heterotopia: specific functions with specific temporalities constructed other territories that were distinguished clearly within the city and the territory (Foucault, 1984). But the progressive fragmentation of urban space has made the whole of the city and the territory resemble a campus. However paradoxical it may seem, land design has become all the more important the more the fragmentation of urban space has become generalized.

Once again there are many projects that have followed these two lines of research in recent years; considering them not opposite but complementary directions that can be amalgamated or not, and that have revealed the significance of the land and the richness of its design.

Both lines of research, and land design in general, seek to transform a topography into a topology, into sequences of recognizable places that are able to convey the sense of an urban space: the sense, not the function and not even the role. The functions housed in Siena's Piazza del Campo have changed radically on more than one occasion over time, and so has the role played by the square in the social and economic life of the Sienese, but it has not changed its sense with respect to the entire urban structure, with respect to the mental map of the Sienese and of visitors to Siena.

J.D. Hunt, *L'art du jardin et son histoire*, Editions Odile Jacob, Paris 1996.
B. Secchi, *Prima lezione di Urbanistica*, Laterza, Roma 2000.
F. Choay, *Espacements. L'évolution de l'espace urbain en France*, Skira, Milan-Geneva 2003.
P. Viganò, *La città elementare*, Skira, Milan 1999.

M. Foucault, 'Des espaces autres', in *Architecture, Mouvement, Continuité*, no. 5, Oct. 1984 (now in: *Dits et écrits*, Gallimard, Paris, 1994); Eng. trans: 'Of Other Spaces', in *Diacritics*, vol. 16, no. 1 (Spring 1986).

R. Venturi and D. Scott
Brown, Basco Showroom,
Philadelphia, 1979

Figures

There has always been a rhetorical component to public space. In fact the functionality of these spaces permits a freer form of representativeness than that of private spaces, and one that tends to make use of a series of figures with a powerful impact, almost slogans for public consumption.

In its iconoclastic enthusiasm the early Modern Movement set out to curb what could be considered a drift toward expressive chaos at the time. So representativeness was relegated to a few objects of art set up in public places. If we think of Mies's Barcelona Pavilion or the square in front of his Seagram Building, the concept is clear in both situations: the architecture serves as the backdrop for a representative figure, statues in these particular cases.

The advent of mass culture has radically modified the nature and perception of public space. So for once architects had to turn their backs on the logic of the Modern Movement in order to learn from Las Vegas about a world made of signs and their continual hybridization with architecture. With their famous book dedicated to that cacophonous but stimulating city, Robert Venturi and Denise Scott-Brown in fact drew up the frame of reference in which the current culture of public space has developed. In their view, however, the sequence of signs was absorbed by the places and buildings in a literal sense, as direct citation. But what has happened in the decades since then has been a further elaboration, which has moved from literal citation towards something more complex and structured. Thus the figures of today's non-volumetric architecture are products of synthesis, more and more a hybrid of abstract culture, Pop imagery and the icons of modern architecture.

Bridges Glanerbeek

2003-2005
Glanerbrug, Enschede,
Netherlands

The bridge at Enschede is conceived with a deck that has gaps between the different lanes of traffic, for pedestrians, bicycles and buses, in order to establish a direct relationship with the river beneath. The structure is built of blocks of stone held together by metal cages and of continuous framework.

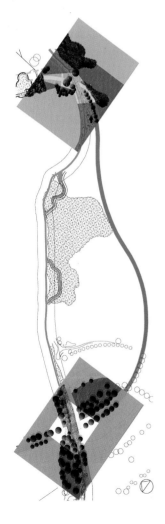

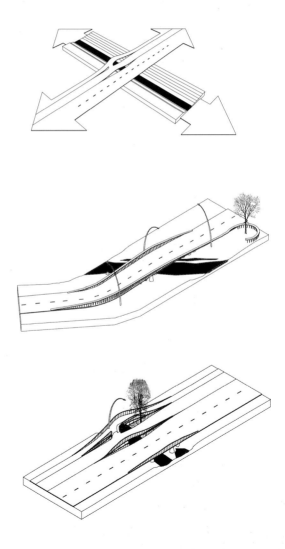

Circle Path

2001-2004
Museumbos Almere,
Netherlands

The idea of the Circle Path is to allow walkers to see the green space that surrounds them from different points of view. The large circle has a diameter of 100 metres and, starting from a level of 3 metres below ground, rises to a height of 35 metres above the countryside. As a result, walking along the path is like making a journey through the different levels of the trees, from the roots to the crown.

Christian de
Portzamparc

Water Tower – The green Tower

1971-1974
Marne-La Vallée, France

The tower dominates an urbanized valley on the outskirts of Paris and is located on a traffic island at the junction of two busy roads. The tower is thirty metres high and is a concrete lattice with a metal-grid facing that rises in a spiral from a height of seven metres above ground. Over the course of time, climbing plants have covered the facing.
The spiral movement of the facing and the dimensions of the object, contrasting with the surrounding suburban buildings, bestow a monumental quality on the tower, making it look like a Tower of Babel clothed in greenery.

Nascent Terrain

2005
Culver City,
California, Usa

Nascent Terrain is a project for the reconversion of a series of industrial lots, degraded by a succession of sheds and car parks constructed over time without the minimum attention being paid to the space in which they are set. With the aim of revitalizing the area by salient points, the project sets out to transform a series of nondescript buildings into a dynamic composition, organized on the principle of the green campus, a connective tissue of vegetation that comes together in a true central courtyard. Thus the courtyard becomes the backdrop of the new architectural landscape, made up of operations of restyling that emphasize particular points of the existing anonymous buildings.

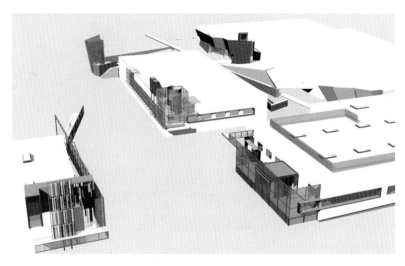

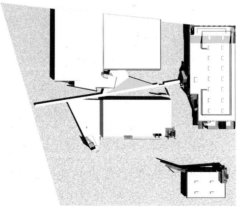

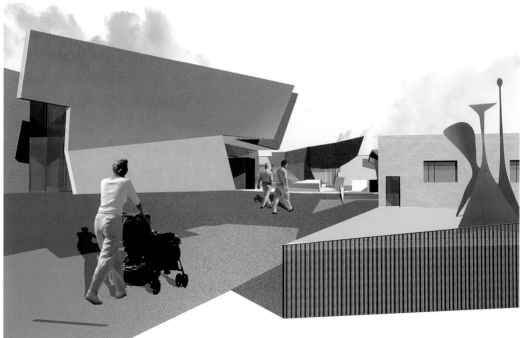

Hild und K   **Gold-Containers**

1996
Landshut, Germany

With the separate collection of household waste the spaces where skips are located have increased in size considerably, and this only serves to augment the sensation of squalor produced by these spaces. The Gold-Containers project sets out to create a decorous space in which to house the skips, based on the use of a simple enclosure. As well as accommodating the enclosure for the separate collection of household waste, the Gold-Container is linked at one end to a bus stop and at the other to a small processing plant. The whole structure is built out of simple prefabricated concrete slabs, assembled on site and painted a golden colour.

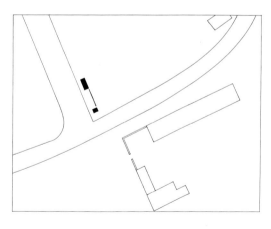

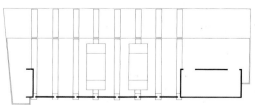

Garofalo Architects   **Stolon Projects**

1999
Chicago, Illinois, Usa

The Stolon Projects for Chicago are architectural visions whose aim is to enrich the city centre with genuine installations. The concept is that of micro-town-planning: a series of interventions that are contained but have a powerful impact, creating what amounts to a monumentality on a reduced scale. The installations utilize art and digital effects to present the image of a hypothetical city of participation.

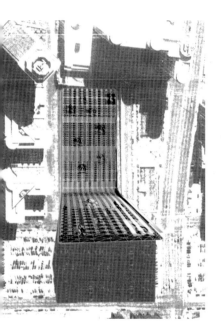

MCA. Beetwen the Museum and the City

2003
Chicago, Illinois, Usa

The MCA Temporary Structure has been erected at the entrance of the Museum of Contemporary Art in Chicago as a reflection on public space, in the hypothesis that a museum should also be an experiential work of architecture, liveable and available to all, especially on the outside.

Rémy Marciano

Extension in Marseille

2001
Marseilles, France

The project consists of a single element, an all-enveloping facing that provides a setting for a building and that, detaching itself from it, creates an open-air patio. The idea is to seek a relationship of resemblance between the building and its surroundings, as if the dimension and form of the cladding were the moment at which the existing enclosure and the adjacent park found their point of synthesis. So the facing becomes a camouflage consisting of sheet metal with a repeated pattern of tiny holes, halfway between the abstract and the naturalistic.

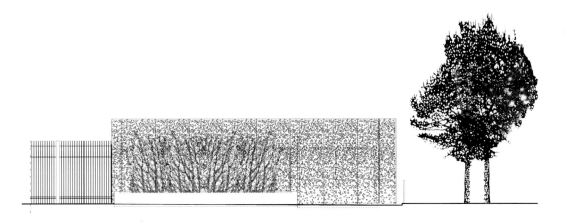

Vertical garden

1999
Rome, Italy

There was not enough space to make a garden on the ground, so the decision was taken to create a vertical one, which could also serve as a piece of urban scenery and an important visual signal for anyone arriving by car. The base of the vertical garden is constructed of rough-hewn travertine, on which is set a system of terraces realized with a metal structure. On the north side the structure supports a series of large copper-clad tubs used to hold the soil. The tubs are planted with jasmine, ivy and honeysuckle, which flower in different seasons. On the south side will be set a wall of glass panes to channel rainwater to the foot of the structure for irrigation.

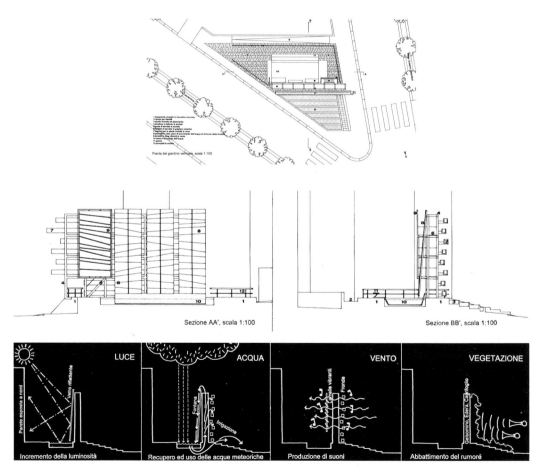

Pianta del giardino verticale, scala 1:100

Sezione AA', scala 1:100

Sezione BB', scala 1:100

LUCE — Incremento della luminosità

ACQUA — Recupero ed uso delle acque meteoriche

VENTO — Produzione di suoni

VEGETAZIONE — Abbattimento del rumore

Frederic Schwartz
Architects

The Hoboken September 11th Memorial

2001
Hoboken, NY, Usa

Hoboken lost 57 of its citizens in the tragedy of 11 September. The monument
is intended not only to commemorate the dead, but also Hoboken and its relationship
with Lower Manhattan. The idea is that of the living memorial, of a place not just
to be looked at, but also walked on. A rationalistic framework positioned on a pier
in the sea suspends a series of walkways that rise gently. The frame is made
of stainless steel and serves to focus the gaze on the place where the Twin Towers
stood. At night a diffuse lighting emphasizes the movement of the people
climbing the walkway.

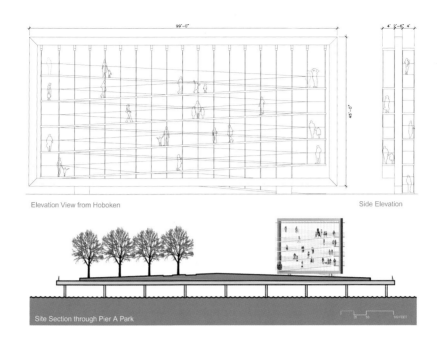

99'-0"

45'-0"

4' 2'-6" 4'

Elevation View from Hoboken

Side Elevation

Site Section through Pier A Park

25   50   100 FEET

the empty space' of squares, roads, public spaces, the landscape. The second has a more remote and conceptual character, and is rooted in a series of events, reflections and projects that have emerged following the crisis of 'postmodernity', that have begun to accustom us to the idea of a dematerialized architecture, and therefore one that has been stripped of some of its atavistic myths of foundation, be they caves, huts or shelters woven out of branches. This conceptual workshop of the 'dematerialization' of architecture is certainly one of the essential premises for the current spread and success of zero-volume works of architecture.[1] And it is also the question to which I would like to devote this short essay, seeking to point out, in the current tendency towards an architecture of emptiness, the elements of continuity with those premises and the traces of meaning that can throw the most light on the present relations between architecture and the complicated spirit of our time.

Why Jacques Derrida makes such good buildings?

In 1986, Bernard Tschumi, winner of the competition for the Parc de La Villette, invited Peter Eisenman and Jacques Derrida to draw up a proposal for one of the gardens located along the *promenade cinématique* around which his project was organized. Eisenman was at that moment the guru of conceptual architecture, made 'of paper' and founded on absence, officially the enemy of the form *d'auteur*. Derrida was the philosopher-father of the post-modern, the man who got us used to the idea of the 'disappearance of the text', the only one capable of giving some substance to the concept of 'deconstruction'[2], so loved and abused by architects in those years. The opportunity was alluring, a sort of perfect alchemy: Tschumi, on whose work Derrida had turned his critical attention in the past, had just come up with the perfect post-modern project for the park of La Villette: he had simply mapped and transferred onto the area of the abattoir of Paris – explained Eisenman himself – the abstract grid that Le Corbusier had drawn up for the Cannaregio area in Venice, also close to a slaughterhouse. On the points marked out by the grid Tschumi placed follies, conspicuous forms virtually devoid of internal space (or indifferent to it). The 'programme' shoves it inside the volumes of the old, slightly altered building and holds the whole thing together with a canopy-sculpture stretching for several hundred meters, running right through the park and leading to the ugly Musée de la Science. In essence and well-ahead of its time, this delineates the absolute archetype of 'zero-volume architecture' and is certainly one of the points of no return in the history of architectural thought and contemporary urban design.

Even when the perfect alchemical formula has been found, as the novelists of the 19th century were well aware, there is no guarantee that it is going to yield gold. On the contrary, *Why Peter Eisenman Writes Such Good Books'* is the ironic title of Derrida's essay published in the book[3] that tells the story of their project for La Villette. Eisenman sought a hermetic and hyper-conceptual, deliberately uninhabitable result; Derrida wanted a design that would be simple to use, a clear and meaningful 'sculpture'. Peter's desire for power was obviously more assertive and disenchanted, and

in the end steered the collaboration in the direction of a strange spa-
tiotemporal puzzle, a spatially unresolved design that would never be realized. But what interests us here is not so much the specific quality of
the project as the reasoning that brings to light the virtuous resonances
between Eisenman's experimentation and Derrida's theoretical approach,
the precedents that had generated them, making possible one of those rare
moments of cosmic ecstasy in which architecture coincides perfectly with
the history of thought.

By then Eisenman had already shown ample signs of fully understanding
what architecture could be at the time of the disappearance of the text,
at the end of the 20th century. Tafuri was obviously well aware of this when
he chose to open the part of his book-catalogue *Five Architects NY* devoted to the architect from New York who is so passionately fond of Terrag-
ni with a striking image taken from an essay by Eisenman published by
the IAUS in 1970, *Notes on Conceptual Architecture*: '[...] four white sheets,
devoid of text, on which Eisenman has arranged 15 numbered dots cor-
responding to the same number of footnotes, filled with references to
Minimal Art, Conceptual Art, Chomsky's transformational linguistics,

Peter Eisenman,
competition project
for the area of San Giobbe,
Cannaregio, Venice, Italy,
1978

Panofsky's iconology [...]. That unwritten article chimes perfectly with the sense of his architecture. *Absence* of architectural "discourse" and ascetic rigour, verging on fanaticism, in the construction of that absence'.[4] OK, but these are still just 'good books', Derrida would say. Yet Eisenman had also managed to transfer his concept precisely into an earlier and much more successful architectural project than that of La Villette, the competition entry for the area of Cannaregio in Venice, another example of the transformation of 'zero-volume' urban space founded on the reclamation of the grid (once again) traced there by Corbu and brutally 'dismissed' from the minds of architects and the city. The architecture of the following years, which has never denied owing a great deal to Peter Eisenman's research, was then transcribed in more immediate critical terms: discontinuity, instability, collage, catastrophe, the uncanny and a thousand other declensions of deconstructionist and late-modern aesthetics. However, there can be no doubt that nothing has undermined the idea of architecture as instrument and raw material of the foundation of urban space as we knew it more than that short series of Eisenman's projects, Tschumi's 'Parc and the conceptual bombardment to which the group of architects and thinkers engaged at La Villette – let us not forget that Koolhaas came up with a project very similar to Tschumi's – subjected the idea of architectural 'discourse'.

Conceptual vs. void

The conceptual utopia so well represented in those projects[5] (one thinks of the Wexner Center, of Libeskind's Jewish museum, of Coop Himmelb(l)au's addition of extra storeys to a building in Vienna), dissolved over the following years into two equally utopian currents, still protagonists of Kurt Forster's last insipid Biennale.[6] On the one hand the digital utopia, with its attempt to construct space directly from post-Euclidean geometry, leapfrogging the tectonic phase, and on the other the obsession with design of the 'ground', which has become a speciality in itself and that suddenly began to rise, swell, move, undulate and open up, offering us infinite and highly complicated variations on the sublime disposition produced by Gabetti and Isola 35 years ago for the residence of Olivetti researchers at Ivrea. Both of them cases, however, in which the volume is anything but equal to zero and which, above all, end up focusing on an obsessive search for the 'form' that the early conceptual projects knew how to let arise with splendid naturalness from the 'process'.

For all these reasons, and because of my own cultural background, when the authors of this book asked me to write an article on the subject of zero-volume architecture, my first reaction was to go back to the experience of conceptual architecture, seen as an essential antecedent to the current interest in 'design of the void'. The second was to verify my hypothesis by looking at how much of that cultural formulation was still present in the projects selected by Aldo Aymonino and Valerio Mosco for this book. I uncovered different answers, some of them consistent with my hypothesis, others indicative of a more distant criterion. In general what I found was a selection based on an idea slightly divergent (and certainly more wide-ranging) than what I have described. The complex taxonomy expounded by the authors seems in fact to refer above all to the idea of works of architecture that in the majority of cases float in the void, occupying the space of nature, the city or infrastructure with the force of an event and turning it into the location of a negotiation between humanity and urban density, humanity and the rarefied space of nature, humanity and the monumental force of infrastructures. Parks, streets, more or less enclosed gardens, bus stops, promenades, junctions, bridges, markets, shelters and canopies of various kinds are generally located on sites awaiting a plan, or else left to the self-determination of nature or urban dynamics. In these cases the legacy of conceptual architecture, if that is what we can call it, lies perhaps in the surprising formal autonomy of these spaces, which no longer arise by continuity and deduction from the relationship with the urban fabrics or with the form of the places or infrastructures, but almost always answer to a strong and self-referential inner logic, clearly based on a 'concept' that the designer wants to convey in the space. It suffices to think of the projects of the studio EMBT, of those of West 8, of Coop Himmelb(l)au's towers for the Swiss Expo, of Zucchi's Gratosoglio, of Martha Schwartz's Whitehead Institute and of the bridges of the Granda studio in order to see that the physical identity of these projects does not derive from the form of the context but from the relationship that the author intends to establish with its deepest nature and with the whole range of possible reactions on the part of the visitor or the passer-by. Less common, but equally exemplary, however, are the projects that take us more directly back to the realm of conceptual action as it has been codified by its originators. They are projects that almost always start out from a well-defined spatial, architectural or urban identity and then go on to alter it, comment on it, contaminate it and subject it to stress. Striking examples of this are the projects of Vito Acconci, not coincidentally a former conceptual artist and now an architect of urban events, those of Decq and Cornette, some of the urban proposals of Wes Jones, Diller and Scofidio's cloud, Burri's crack obviously and several others, which almost never start out from the need to 'create space', but from that of 'producing meaning'.

Parasite architecture

At the end of the nineties Peter Eisenman's favourite pupil at the time, Greg Lynn, designed and realized the Korean Presbyterian Church in the New York borough of Queens. This was an intervention of digital architecture on an existing building: the spaces of the religious complex remained more or less the same, but were traversed by an invasive and recognizable parasite that appeared on the outside of the building, definitively modifying its meaning and overall appearance. It is a crystalline example of 'zero-volume conceptual architecture', the translation into metal girders and panels of that fusion of conceptual architecture and digital philosophy to which Eisenman's early heirs aspired. Unfortunately the experiment was not a great success. The building communicates very little and has nothing of the organic and purist abstraction that pervades the authors' fascinating computer graphics. It is immediately apparent that the digital will have a future closer to sculpture than to urban transformation and that the necessary techniques of construction are still too sophisticated and costly to be widely used. One intention remains, however: that of thinking of the project as a 'parasite' within the body of the existing work of architecture and city. In my view this may emerge as one of the 'critical' cases of zero-volume architecture, and in particular the one closest to its postmodern and conceptual philosophical origin.

I find this assertion more important than ever in the scenario of the transformation of European cities and landscapes, afflicted by millions of cubic meters of disused industrial buildings, hundreds of new towns in which no-one wants to live any longer, endless districts to be 'upgraded', stations to be moved and structures to be recycled and uninhabitable infrastructural areas, which it is often too expensive to demolish and rebuild and pointless to 'renovate' without a more radical alteration of the nature of the architectural container and above all its perception in society. Putting together the concepts of zero volume, conceptual architecture and architectural parasitism, I then set out to propose a form of architectural recycling that seems to me to be particularly suited to the necessities and spirit of contemporary space. Necessary because, at least in the West, it is inevitable that we should think about architecture in terms of the economy of space and resources, and of refinement of the techniques that allow us to make the best possible use of the infinite *cadavres exquis* that the city discovers within its boundaries on a daily basis. Opportune because it also permits us to take a step forwards and settle for once and for all the hoary discussion about the language of architecture and the role of representation that some want it to have, while others want it to be one of pure communication, and still others one of scenery. If we think of the identity of the bodies riddled with architectural parasites as the combination of two natures that cannot be summed, that in any case remain separate, it will be precisely the friction/conflict between these two natures (physical, material, functional, conceptual) that will give rise to the code of expression of a building, its capacity to make itself clear to those who have to live in it, look at it and understand its value and role.

The catalogue of examples, as has already been pointed out, is ample and ranges from the heroic projects of Eisenman, Tschumi and Koolhaas (not to go back as far as Mario Fiorentino's house on Via Paisiello) to the cases lined up in this publication. The raw material, made up of the corpses of buildings and disused, obsolete, rejected and inadequate bits of city, is equally abundant and urgently requires a strategy that is not merely the pure and depressing habit of 'reuse', a practice that does not allow design the right to a face that belongs to its own age.

[1] It suffices to think of the success attained in recent times by an 'author' like Vito Acconci, well represented in this book. In the transfer of his work from the pure realm of conceptual art to the hybrid one of architecture (via public art), Acconci is doing nothing but theorize continually on the myriad operations that can be carried out in (urban) space without 'constructing' in the traditional sense: warping, adding, penetrating, piercing, transfixing, etcetera.

[2] '[...] a general positioning of its motifs for architectural design: do not destroy; maintain, renew, and reinscribe. Do battle with the very meaning of architectural meaning without proposing a new order...' J. Kipnis on Jacques Derrida in 'Twisting the Separatrix,' in *Assemblage*, no. 14 (April 1991), now in K. Michael Hays (ed.) *Architectural Theory since 1968*, MIT press, Cambridge (Mass.), 1998, p. 710.

[3] J. Kipnis and T. Leeser (eds.), *Chora L Works. Jacques Derrida and Peter Eisenman*, Monacelli Press, New York 1993.

[4] M. Tafuri, 'Les bijoux indiscrets', in Id., *Five Architects N.Y.*, Officina Edizioni, Rome 1981.

[5] Philip Johnson and Mark Wigley (curators), *Deconstructivist Architecture*, MOMA, June-August 1988, catalogue published by the MOMA.

[6] *Metamorph*, 9th International Exhibition of Architecture, Venice Biennale, September-November 2004, organized by Kurt Forster. Catalogue published by Marsilio, Venice 2004.

G. Schuchov, Tower
of Shabolouka radio
station, Mosca 1922

Technology

Technology is playing an ever greater part in our daily lives. It has two faces: on the one hand the hard technologies connected with infrastructure networks, on the other the soft technology of electronics and immaterial systems. While hard technology has a direct impact on the territory, soft technology finds expression through effects that are less physically evident but so invasive that they redefine the already fragile borderline between what is public and what is private.

As was already pointed out at the time by critics like Giedion and Zevi, the fascination of technical artefacts was one of the central elements in the development of the style of the early Modern Movement. The images of steel pylons that reached their lyrical apogee in the works of Schuchov were to all intents and purposes one of the aesthetic prototypes for the generation of the masters. Subsequently, technical design lost its initial creative impetus and fell back on a mechanical standardization of its elements.

In the contemporary world we are seeing a renewed aesthetic interest in the design of technical artefacts. The results are still not up to expectations. The formal definition of the elements, in fact, has remained the prerogative of a repetitive approach to design that, for reasons of safety and cost, still remains distrustful of aesthetic motivations. Discussion of the design of technical artefacts is further complicated by the fact that it appears increasingly to be caught between the comprehensible but limiting causes of anonymity and a desire for ever more plastic form, verging on expressionism, which is probably valid when the element is a one-off piece, but wholly inappropriate in the congenital repetitiveness of technical works of architecture.

Martinez Lapeña
Elia Torres

Esplanada Fórum 2004

2001-2004
Barcelona, Spain

In the Plan Cerdá of 1858, the Avenida Diagonal ended up in a vague empty space without reaching the sea. The Explanada del Forum sets out to provide the Avenida Diagonal with the access to the sea that it had never had. This outlet consists of an esplanade in the form of an open hand covering an area of 14 hectares that slopes down to the sea.

The paving of the open hand takes the form of a gigantic patchwork of asphalt in five colours. The paving is a technological surface beneath which run the services. On the esplanade stand 'pleated' pergolas and a pergola of photovoltaic cells with an area of 4500 m², sloping to the south at an angle of 35 degrees. From a distance the pergolas look like yet another construction in the industrial landscape of Barcelona.

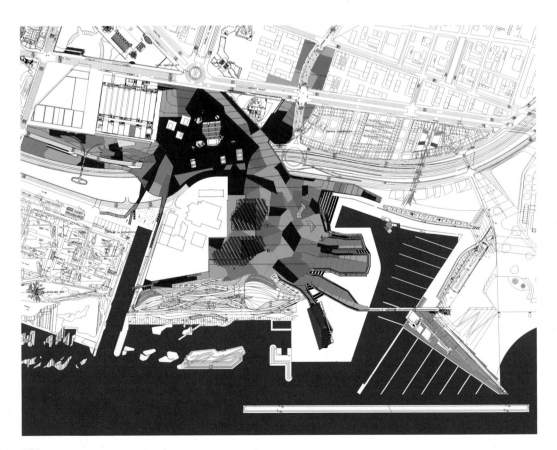

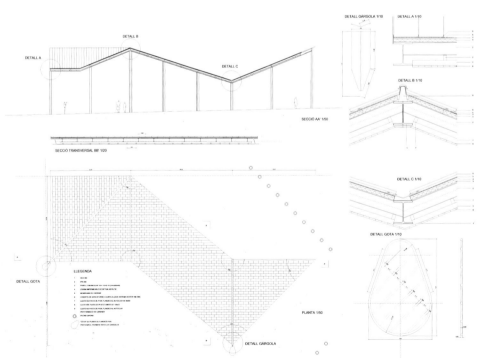

DETALL GÀRGOLA 1/10   DETALL A 1/10

DETALL B

DETALL A   DETALL C

SECCIÓ AA' 1/50

SECCIÓ TRANSVERSAL BB' 1/20

DETALL B 1/10

LLEGENDA

DETALL GOTA

DETALL C 1/10

DETALL GOTA 1/10

PLANTA 1/50

DETALL GÀRGOLA

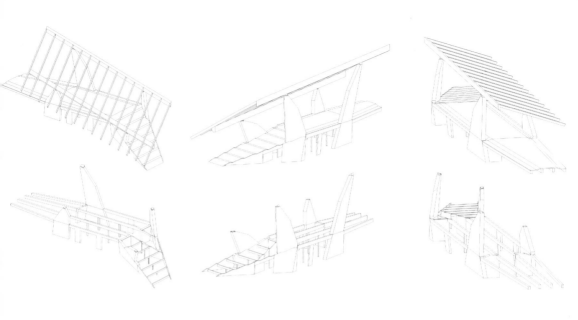

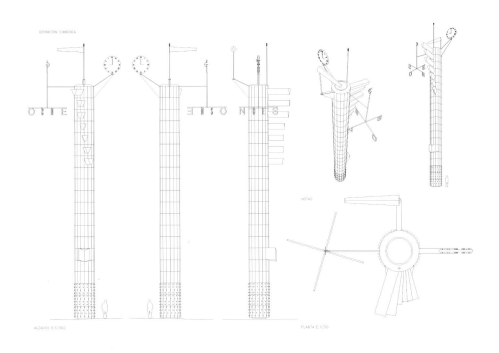

DEFINICIÓN CHIMENEA

VISTAS

ALZADOS E.1/100   PLANTA E.1/50

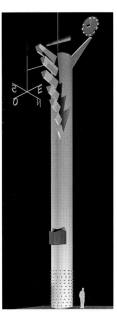

Achille Castiglioni
Michele De Lucchi

High-tension Pylons

1999

The idea was to come up with a pylon that would not be a traditional lattice.
So the designers worked on transforming the lattice into a tensile structure made up of eight identical bars that function as struts or ties.
Lightness and transparency are the fundamental concepts behind an object that keeps its impact on the landscape to a minimum. This is combined with ease of assembly and the obvious economic advantages of a construction made up of identical pieces.

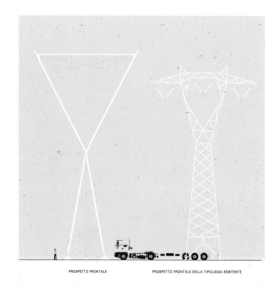

PROSPETTO FRONTALE   PROSPETTO FRONTALE DELLA TIPOLOGIA ESISTENTE

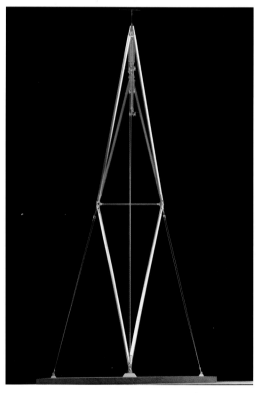

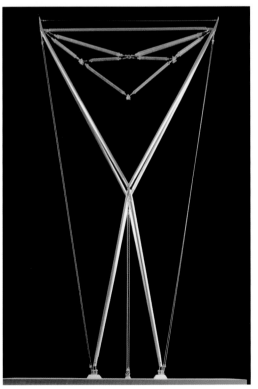

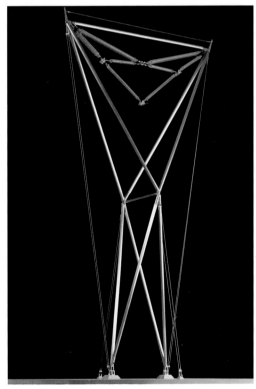

High-tension Pylons

1999

The pylon is about 60 metres high and 10 wide and is characterized by a butterfly shape, made up of eight prefabricated components in galvanized steel that form two arms. The arms approach one another as they rise and then diverge again at the top, where they support the triad of cables. The structure of the pylon is very light and is designed to adapt itself to differences in the level of the ground. The principle of the pylon is that of a filigreed structure, with little visual impact on the surroundings.

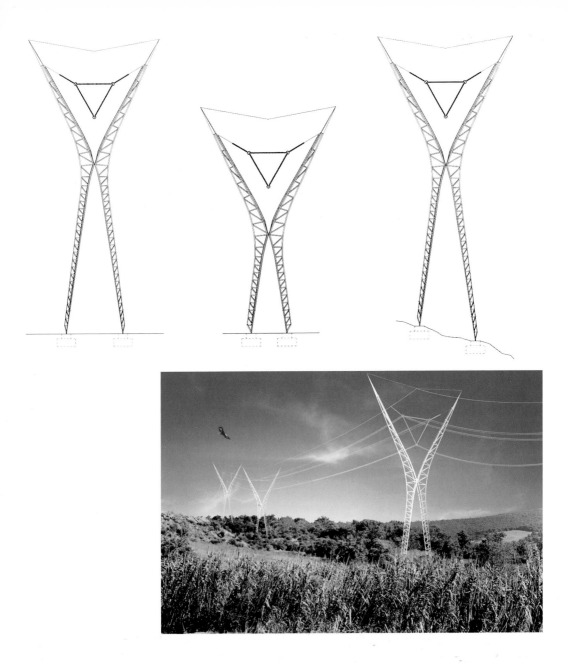

Aldo Aymonino

Hogh-tension Pylon

1999

The design proposal is based on a simple geometry, capable of providing both an efficient and resistant structure that is not too complicated from the viewpoint of statics, and an image that attempts to make the form and design of the industrial pylon more plastic and supple than the ones currently in production. The structure is formed out of steel tubes of standard sizes, with a diameter of 508 mm for the main structure and one of 101.6 mm for the secondary one, linked transversally by three elements that support the electrical system, constructed in the assembly shop with a structure formed out of cold-bent HEB 100 girders.

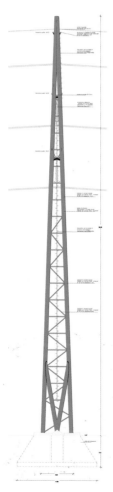

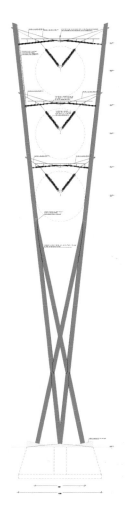

Claus En Kaan — **Entrance Building to Waste Water Treatment System (DWR Entrée)**

2003-2005
Rhijnspoorplein
Amsterdam,
Netherlands

This technical work of architecture is designed to distinguish the entrance of Amsterdam's Waste Water Treatment System. It is located on a highly visible site, in the vicinity of a busy road close to the city centre. Technically, the object is a reinforced-concrete air inlet for the underground technical plant, but adds to this function a powerful sculptural image, which twists dynamically on itself.

Touch of Evil

2002-2004
Pijnacker, Netherlands

"What happened here? On the walls and ceilings of the tunnel a strange imprint is visible. A big, whimsical and brightly coloured imprint, an imprint of an unreal and immeasurable shape. As if during the building an unearthly thing got stuck between the formwork. As if the soul of the former landscape, being rooted up by bulldozer, has gone underground. As if the winding pattern of old polder roads, which has made place for rigid urban developments, takes revenge in the tunnel". (Maurice Nio)

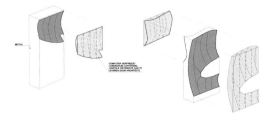

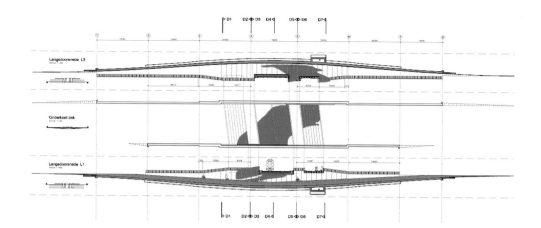

Portland Aerial Tram

2003
Portland, Usa

The area where the terminal is located is physically detached from the rest of the
urban fabric by an ever increasing number of highways, exit ramps and layouts
of every kind. So the idea is to overcome these obstacles with all sorts of connections,
from an elevated one by means of a cableway, another cableway on the ground
and a footbridge, elements that taken altogether define an architectural landscape.
Through the presence of these deliberately odd structures, an attempt has been
made to characterize a nondescript and congested sector of the city.

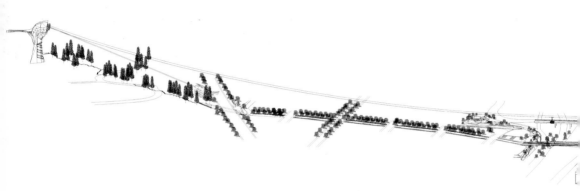

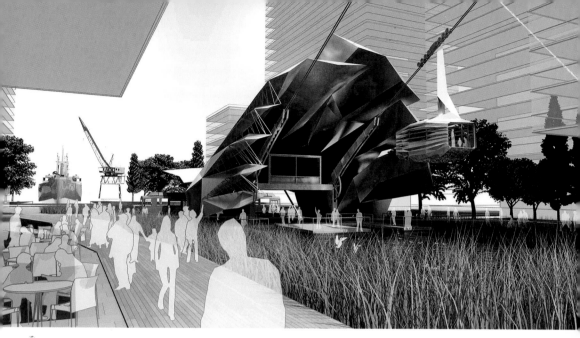

Struijs
Public Works
Rotterdam

Wind Barriers

1983-1985
Rotterdam, Netherlands

The project is situated in the vicinity of the port of Rotterdam and is composed on a territorial scale of a series of simple reinforced-concrete elements organized according to the logic of repetition. In this case the technical landscape appears timeless, as if suspended between memories of the ruins of fortified cities and images of major works of infrastructure in reinforced concrete.

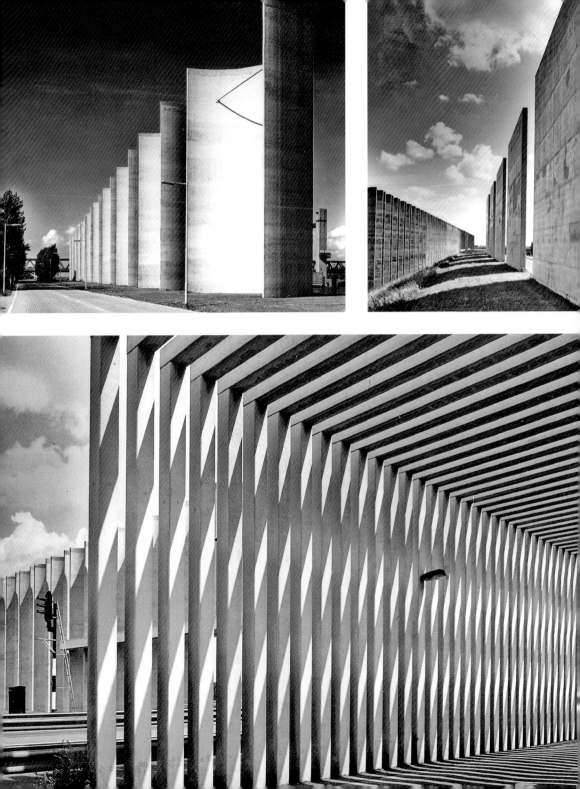

Piezometric Tower at Codigoro, Water Lifting Plant

2003-2004
Polesine Ferrarese, Italy

One of the most problematic aspects of the lifting plant in Valle Giralda was its proportions, dictated by inescapable technical necessities; the structure, in fact, is as high as the upper basin is wide. Adding the pipes and the lifts and an observation platform to the upper basin, there was a risk that the whole thing would look ungainly and have a negative impact on the surroundings. So it was decided first of all to break up the volume of the upper tank into several sections, in order to make the whole thing look more slender and permit the rays of the sun to pass through the suspended volume. To this is added the definition of the basin at ground level, so that it can serve as a public park.

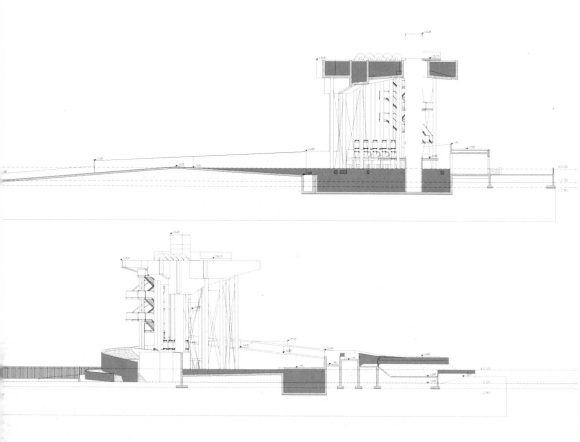

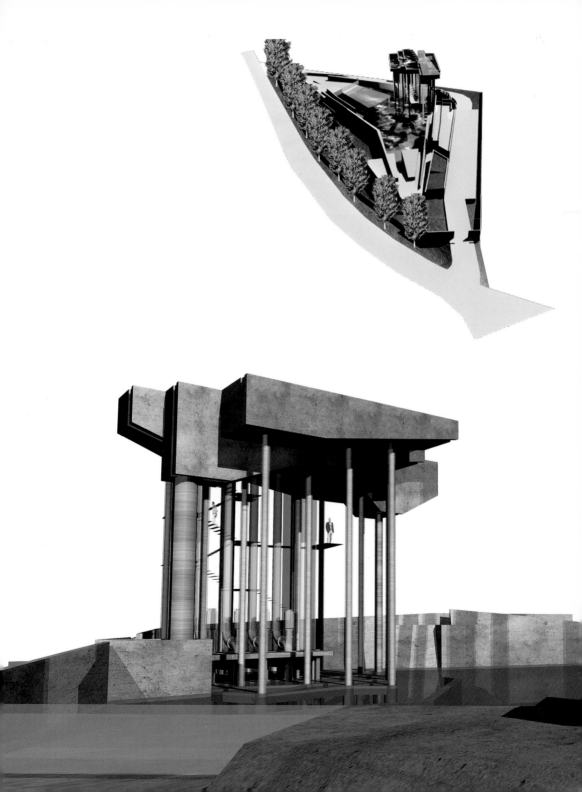

ONL Oosterhuis
Lénárd

Acoustic Barrier

2005
Leidsche Rijn, Utrecht,
Netherlands

Acoustic barriers alongside busy roads are usually intrusive and anonymous objects, made up of mechanically repeated elements. When all is said and done they lack design, the formal value that elevates functionality to the level of an aesthetic experience. In this case an attempt has been made to go beyond designs out of the catalogue, configuring an *ad hoc* object that owes its form precisely to the fluid dynamism suggested by the layouts of the infrastructure. The barrier is then even treated as a means of generating the architecture behind it.

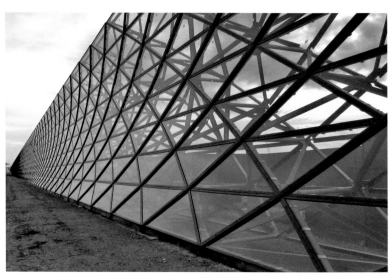

Giuseppe Vele

System for the collection of rainwater in Baku

2003
Baku, Azerbaijan

The project sets out to define an alternative system for the collection of rainwater. It is a structure in the shape of an upturned umbrella constructed out of very lightweight materials, such as PVC, Teflon and nylon. The membrane that forms the umbrella has a cavity between the upper and lower surface which is filled with helium. The entire structure is supported in the air at a height that varies according to piezometric requirements. The layout allows water to be transported around the territory in a completely natural way, without the aid of mechanical systems. To obtain an even greater equilibrium there is a system of anchorage to the ground by means of steel cables.

FASI DI GONFIAGGIO

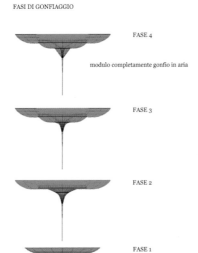

FASE 4

modulo completamente gonfio in aria

FASE 3

FASE 2

FASE 1

modulo sgonfio a terra

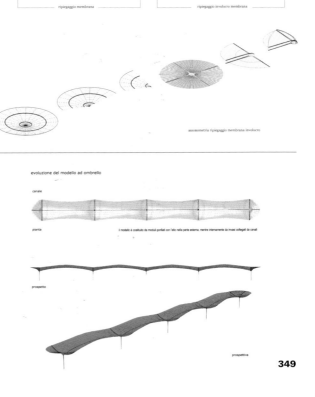

ripiegaggio membrana

ripiegaggio involucro membrana

assonometria ripiegaggio membrana involucro

evoluzione del modello ad ombrello

canale

pianta

Il modello è costituito da moduli gonfiati con l'elio nella parte esterna, mentre internamente da invasi collegati da canali

prospetto

prospettiva

349

E66 Wind turbine

1993

Turbines for the production of wind power have to be able marry the demands of efficiency with the need to reduce the impact on the environment. A wind turbine has three main components, the blades, the generator and the supporting shaft, which have to be harmonized into a unitary aerodynamic design. The blades are made of fibreglass and epoxy compounds, while the shaft is constructed of steel elements assembled on site. The mast is 100 metres high and the blades have a diameter of 66 metres. With an output of 1.8 megawatts, each turbine can generate enough energy for 1500 homes.

A Light Windmill Mast

1999

The design aims to make the structure as light and stable as possible and at the same time reduce the load on the foundation to a minimum. So the choice fell on a 100-metre-high steel mast, as slender as possible, with a diameter that reaches a maximum of 3 metres, braced halfway-up by a tensile structure with three rows of cables. The mast stands on a hinge fixed to the ground that allows it to be tilted into a vertical position; the mast is then stabilized by the set of stays.

Un-Volumetric Architecture
Arie Graafland

In the 1994-95 *Architecture yearbook*, the Dutch critic Hans van Dijk made the following observation about the then recently completed Groninger Museum by Alessandro Mendini.

"Does the Groninger Museum embody an innovation? Not within the context of established architecture. Apart from the floor plan, which is quite traditional for a museum building, it has nothing to do which what is expected of a museum building. It figures in the architectural discussion as a perversity, an excess or —at best— a birthday cake which very quickly falls victim to the bulimia of the guests. It is not a matter of architecture here. The Groninger Museum embodies the successful infiltration of design into architecture".

To van Dijk, the Groninger Museum introduces nothing new, at least not within the context of established architecture. Apart from the floor plan, the Groninger museum does not look or behave like a museum. It is immodest, seductive, consumerist, not to mention expensive —and it is not recognizable as architecture. It deals with a post-modern sense of leisure. The American literary critic Michael Speaks referring to van Dijk's assessment is of the opposite opinion. Instead of dismissing the Groninger Museum, he claims it to be more accurate (and perhaps less moralistic) to say that the Groninger Museum is so innovative because it cannot be recognized within the context of normal architectural standards. It is no accident that Speaks' defence of the museum starts with an argument from Venturi, who in the 1960s and 70s called for a new relationship between architecture and the commercialism of the Las Vegas 'strip', rendering all 'resistant' architecture —as they called it— ineffective and obsolete. But he also called for a new practice of architecture in which *communication* rather than space would be the essential feature. Along with Denise Scott Brown and Steven Izenour, Venturi argued in *Learning from Las Vegas* that in the early twentieth century space came to dominate all other concerns in architecture. Venturi called for a more flexible practice of architecture which could keep pace with the image-driven consumer culture that had emerged after the war.

Where Speaks is rather optimistic and positive, the German art historian Michael Müller is quite negative and pessimistic. Also referring to Venturi he writes the following: "The realities of architecture and space effectively disappear, giving way to electronically simulated information, advertising, games, gestures and symbols. We can say that the surface of the building has finally emancipated itself from its conventional utility value". Aestheticization as we know it today, has long since reacted to this change. By creating new links between the various media, it makes a major contribution to their renewed enhancement. To illustrate his ideas, Muller gives us the example of that same Groninger Museum by Mendini. What is positive for Michael Speaks is negative for Michael Müller. Speaks' key terminology is about *communication*, the key terms for Müller are *space* and *contemplation*. These are no neutral terms. Speaks' problem is with what he calls "identity": in his opinion many contemporary architects are in search of identity. The problem to his mind is with the term identity itself. In his opinion Mendini lies outside his definition of identity. I think Speaks is mixing up 'identity' and 'essence': architecture indeed does not have an essence. Architectural theories like 'functionalism', 'space theory' or historicism have always tried to find one ruling concept. This goes for renaissance proportion, but also for modernism's notions about space. Works of art or architecture might acquire an 'identity' because of our mistaken analysis that reduces architecture to only one dominant characteristic. The problem is with notions of 'essence'. For Michael Müller the Groninger Museum is an example of architectural 'zapping', it is like skipping TV channels, a notion that is often discussed in post-modern discourse. Theorists of the post-modern often talk of an ideal-type channel hopping MTV viewer who flips through different images at such speed that he or she is unable to chain the signifiers together into a meaningful narrative; only the sensations of the surface are consumed. We have to be careful though: one finds little discussion on the actual experiences and practices of watching television by different groups in different settings. The notion merely functions like it does here, as an instrument for intellectual assessment. It is about boundaries between art and everyday life, the collapse of the hierarchal distinction between high and popular culture; it is about play and high culture.

Müller presents another Dutch museum as the opposite of this zapping. The Bonnefantenmuseum in Maastricht by Aldo Rossi is an example of a different kind of architecture. Unlike Mendini and his colleagues, Rossi transforms the heterogeneous collection of visual attractions into a homogeneous structure. At Groningen life appears to be continuously happy, we can walk around without any risk, from one lovely and perfectly staged identity to the other. The Bonnefantenmuseum is a unique mask, just a very strong architectural word in a so called 'chaotic' world. Where everything is floating, unsure and unstable, Rossi intends to restore our belief in eternal validity, says Müller. Rossi's museum is arguing within the intellectual dimension of auratic architecture. Inside it is logically a classical museum that creates the right conditions for presenting works of art. Whereas the Groninger museum represents a never ending need for communication, the Bonnefanten in Maastricht is a silent architecture. We as visitors are not supposed to communicate with it, —this is an architecture of silence, Müller is certainly right here. Groningen also prohibits us from speaking, but precisely because it talks too much. The Groninger Museum wants to be part of the many languages in post-modern discourse, the Bonnefanten wants to be part of the architectural discourse itself. It is mainly interested in its own offspring and tradition. Rossi and with him the Italian Tendenza group, is certainly not interested in notions of 'communication'.

The picture I am trying to draw here is about the *assessment* of unvolumetric architecture and art. The discussion over the two Dutch museums relies heavily on much broader notions of assessment that have to do with society as a whole. Both museums were part of the worldwide epidemic of museum building in the 1990s. The museum has become the focus of a quasi-religious cult, one that promises immortality of a sort for its subscribers, as the English critic Deyan Sudjic remarks. The art museum in particular has become the only sacred building that the modern world is still capable of building. A persistent emphasis on architectural exhibitionism and technical virtuosity serves to underscore its status as a place dedicated to ritual, set apart from the everyday world. I think Sudjic´s qualification here goes for both museums, the Groninger as well as the Bonnefanten in Maastricht. The Dutch critic Hans van Dijk dismisses the Groninger Museum because it offers only extravaganza in architecture. The American critic Michael Speaks thinks the building is innovative because it cannot be recognized within the context of normal architecture. The German critic Michael Müller dismisses the Groninger Museum since it drowns in its own flows of communication. He is more or less in line with Hans van Dijk who appreciates an autonomous language in architecture. Aldo Rossi's Bonnefanten is not touched by our chaotic world. So the positions in assessment that are starting to become clear are those of *'communication'* and *spectacle* in a world we can no longer control, and that of *auratic* art and *autonomy*, which is not related to communication, but to *contemplation*. So far not much has been said about how these museums deal with their exhibition spaces. What I will argue first is that these assessments of the two Dutch museums will also work for the art world.Conceptual art from the sixties and seventies was about aura and autonomy.

Aldo Rossi, project
for the monument
to the Resistenza
in Cuneo, Italy, 1962

Sol LeWitt, Dan Flavin, Donald Judd, Carl Andre and Barnett Newman were about distance and contemplation. Le Witt in his *Paragraphs on Conceptual Art* claims that art should be conceptual, it is planned in advance, the making is far less important. Sol LeWitt, who never executes any of his works himself, is like an Aldo Rossi in architecture. It is no accident that Frank Gehry recently stated that he was bored with minimalist art spaces with simple geometries, which to his mind said nothing to the spectator. Gehry exalted the type of exhibition space that established an expressive dialogue with the exhibited art. What this dialogue is about he never mentioned. What kind of art works he is referring to is an open question. It probably is not about Sol LeWitt, Barnett Newman or Carl Andre. The conclusion might be that "surface" as a quality of unvolumetric architecture can go both ways; it can be heading for the notion of silence in Zen, and it can go for pop-decoration.

A few years ago the Municipal Museum in Amsterdam opened the exhibition of the English artist Sam Taylor Wood. It was her first large exhibition in Holland. She is probably one of the more acceptable photo artists from England, although Tracy Emin has followed later on. Damien Hirst, Tracey Emin, the Chapman brothers, Sarah Lucas, Fiona Banner and Sam Taylor Wood form a group that that is certainly recognizable as a group that deals in *'communication'* and *spectacle* – categories I just used to describe the Groninger Museum. Their private lives and amounts of alcohol consumed and sexual activities are part of this communication structure. The Young British Artists are strongly supported, if not invented, by the communication expert Charles Saatchi, owner of Saatchi&Saatchi. A lot of artists come from Goldsmith's College, where Scott Lash writes his books on our post modern culture. Saatchi buys *en gros*, stocks his paintings for a while, creates a hype around them, and sells the paintings to the art world again. The works themselves are the opposite of those on contemplation: *Sensation* was the title of Saatchi´s exhibition. *Shock-Art* is about communication, Tracey Emin tells us in her video about her abortions and submits the bed as an entry for the Turner Prize. It was later bought by Madonna, who by the way is an art collector herself. Damien Hirst's *Pharmacy*, a huge installation of a pharmacy, scale one to one, was bought by the Tate Modern. He is no longer the rebel, but the respected artist. Sam Taylor Wood sells her photos for £ 20,000 each in the The White Cube, the gallery owned by her husband. (Nan Goldin sells hers for £ 5,000 each). With her solo exhibition in Amsterdam she entered the circles of respected artists in Holland too. The art world has an immense capacity to absorb any form of art. I have no problem with that, the only thing our critics have not mentioned yet is the question *why* communication is either a bad or a good sign. Why contemplation and abstraction are any better than spectacle and event. The same goes for architecture. It is not enough to show that architecture has historical roots that in the end might function like Jungian archetypes as is the case with Rossi. It is also not enough to show *Sensation*, and so called shock-art, and not ask yourself the question why a century-long standing tradition in modern art of shock is still important in our days. It is certainly not enough to mention that the art world is overruled by the advertising world, a lot of great paintings were made on commission for kings and merchants, money and power have always played an important role.

I do not think that we have a dilemma of the exhibition space at hand, it is the *dilemma of contemplation and spectacle*, the *dilemma of Modernism's space-based morals and Venturi's and Mendini's communicative architecture* that is no longer grounded in notions of space. And in the end it is not even about 'space'. The term is completely redundant, space in itself does not mean a thing as long as we do not define the boundaries of 'space', as Isamu Noguchi argues. It is either about notions of 'experience of space', or about the flow of sensations as in contemporary art and media. *The dilemma is about taste*. Consumption of architecture and lifestyle preferences involve discriminatory judgements, which at the same time identify and render classifiable our own particular judgement of taste to others. And as many sociologists have shown us, 'taste' is no neutral concept. We all belong to Bourdieu's 'new cultural intermediaries' in art, architecture, design, fashion, media, and advertising. We are all busy with the production, marketing and dissemination of symbolic goods. Critical theory tends to be quite negative on our present society and its cultural forms. There is of course a lot to sustain these thoughts, and I do sustain them, but in spite of it I think we should look into the work of artists and architects who have relinquished their commitment to high culture and have adopted an increasingly open attitude towards consumer culture and show a willingness to have truck with other cultural intermediaries, image makers, audiences and publics. The critical line here is a thin one, we can no longer discuss this in terms of groups, genres, or 'avant-gardes', we should not even discuss the makers any more, but only their art works and architectures. Young British Artists in that sense is an advertising strategy by Charles Saatchi; the same is true in present day architecture (and has been for quite a while, I think). I do not think that we have a dilemma of the exhibition space, we have an ongoing dilemma in judgement and taste concerning the artworks *and* the architecture of the museum. Design criteria for architecture will always run parallel with other aesthetic notions, I think its more useful to discuss these connections. Different worlds will become visible, but that is what architecture and art are all about.

SITE, Highway 86,
Vancouver, Canada, 1985

Events

Contemporary public space, that of mass society, is increasingly in need of forms to define and exalt ephemeral events.
It is undeniable in fact that our living together tends to produce situations centring on the aggregation produced by entertainment. Our society of minorities rediscovers its unity during just these events and architecture sets out to give form to this need.
The phenomenon is so inherent to our time that it occasionally occurs without a pre-arranged programme, as a spontaneous colonization of places that are spontaneously adapted for the occasion. Non-volumetric architecture has always shown an interest in open-air performances. Since its origins, the modern movement has produced temporary works of architecture, displaying a particular fascination with this theme. In post-modernity primitivism and the ephemeral have been and continue to be two fundamental references for art and architecture.
The novelty of the last few decades is that there is an increasing desire to somatize these events, almost in the hypothesis, typical of the Pop utopia, of eliminating the distance between design and its use.
The creation of campsites on the old Highway 86 was one of the first works to move in this direction: here the world o which ephemeral architecture is dedicated, that of leisure and entertainment, has been monumentalized for collative use and consumption. Recent non-volumetric events show an increasing tendency to emphasize this component through recourse to forms or mechanisms that immediately express their ephemeral character, such as short-lived works of architecture, with the aim of turning even the architecture itself into a transitory event. Great natural metaphysical spectacles are also events; these too, in fact, have the same ability to communicate with the public at large as do urban events for mass entertainment.

Blur Building

2002
Yverdon-les-Bains,
Switzerland

The Blur Building is one of the pavilions constructed for the Swiss Expo 2002 on Lake Neuchâtel. It is an atmospheric work of architecture that can hold 400 visitors at a time. Measuring 100 by 66 metres, it is conceived around water and its manifestations. The water is pumped from the lake and sprayed to create an artificial mist that turns the image and experience of the pavilion into something vague and rarefied. An atmospheric sensing system registers the weather conditions and regulates the jets of nebulized water to suit them.

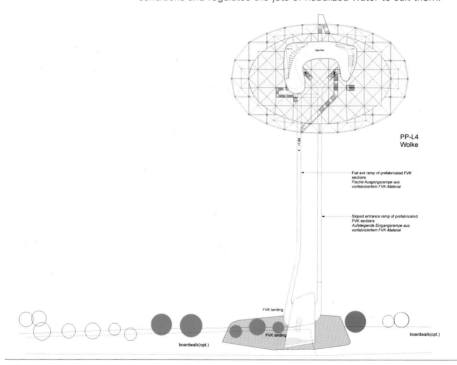

PP-L4
Wolke

Flat exit ramp of prefabricated FVK
sections
Flache Ausgangsrampe aus
vorfabriziertem FVK-Material

Sloped entrance ramp of prefabricated
FVK sections
Aufsteigende Eingangsrampe aus
vorfabriziertem FVK-Material

FVK landing

FVK landing

boardwalk(opt.)

boardwalk(opt.)

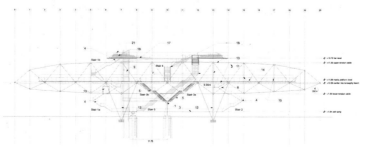

Klein Dytham
Architecture

Pika Pika Pretzel

1999
Harajuku, Tokyo, Japan

Pika Pika Pretzel is an installation located on the street front of a demolished lot in the centre of Tokyo and consists of a six-metre-high inflatable façade risen on a three-metre-high base of sheet metal stretching for thirty-four metres. The material is the same fabric as is used for new high-altitude balloons. The holes serve both to lend rigidity to the structure and to solve the problem of the wind.

Klein Dytham
Architecture

Green Green Screen

2003
Ornotesando, Tokyo,
Japan

The Green Green Screen is also a temporary façade, but this time based on the principle of the wall of plants; a genuine organic enclosure, almost a patchwork that integrates vegetation and graphics with floral motifs. The result is something halfway between natural and artificial decoration.

Franken Architekten   **Take Off – Spatial installation in Terminal II at Munich Airport**

2002
Munich, Germany

The installation is set in the departure lounge of Munich airport, a large hall measuring 200 by 150 metres. The intention is to bring the dynamic and fluid sensation of flight into this hall, ultimately with the aim of preparing travellers psychologically for their coming journey. The structure is composed of 360 different blades with the profile of a wing, which are arranged in a parametric design. It is the movement of the passengers around this sculpture that determines the constantly shifting points of view, in a continuous narrative that takes the form of a kinetic event, where the sensation of dynamism is effectively conjured up without the object having to move.

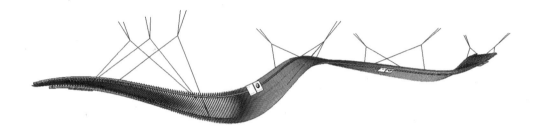

Dominique Perrault   **Milan 2001, Luminous sign**

1999
Milan, Italy

The aim of this luminous sign, set up in the square in front of Milan's Stazione
Centrale, is to create a walk-through sculpture that could also serve as a new gate
for the city. After getting off the train, people pass through two thin walls
of unbreakable glass and aluminium that have the appearance of a playful sculpture
in the daytime and an urban beacon at night. The same glass is used for brace
the walls with lateral partitions. The structure is permeable to the wind
and the lighting systems are of the industrial type, fitted with suitable filters.

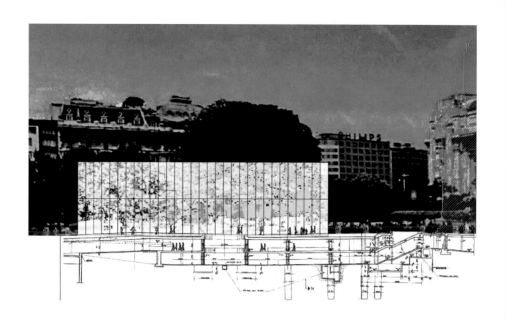

U2, Popmart

1997-1998

Towards the end of the seventies the rock concert became a multimedia event
at which the staging acquired an ever greater importance. The imagery of the stages
designed by the Fisher studio was inspired by certain ideas first put forward
by Archigram's Instant City. The stages of concerts held by the Rolling Stones
and U2 became true works of kinetic architecture with different configurations
that could be dismantled and reassembled on tour in less than 48 hours. In this
connection Mark Fisher considers rock stages to be "[...] the ultimate expression
of un-volumetric architecture".

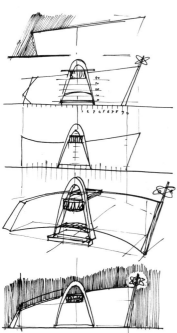

Mark Fisher

Rolling Stones, Bridges to Babylon

1997-1998

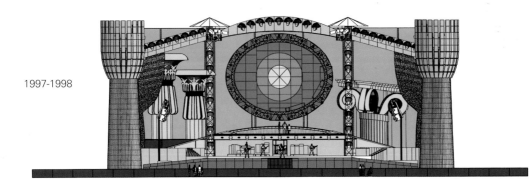

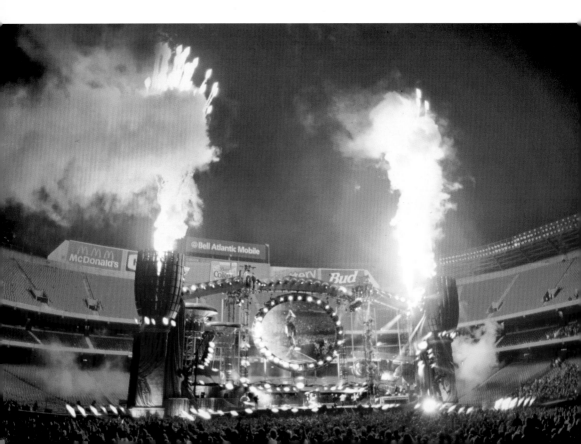

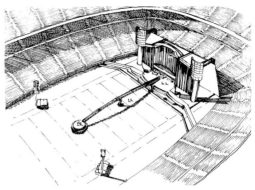

Gerry Judah

Rolls Royce Central Display

2004
Godwood,
Godwood, UK

Gerry Judah's work unites the English tradition of the country fair with the pop festival. The displays are presented as orderly compositions, where a clearly salient point becomes the centre of the event itself, even from a distance. The intention is to combine popular imagery, engineering and a measured dose of ingenuity. In the various Festivals of Speed staged by Judah the theme i s expressed through immediate and easily comprehensible metaphors, to which are added the precision of the high-tech details and a fondness for objects suspended in the air.

Gerry Judah   **Jaguar Central Display**

2000
Godwood, UK

Gerry Judah **Ford Central Display**

2003
Godwood,
UK

Gerry Judah **Renault Central Display**

2002
Godwood,
UK

Pierre Thibault

Jardins d'Hiver

2001
Charlevoix, Québec,
Canada

The winter garden is set in a nature reserve in Quebec, a region of subarctic lakes and forests, and consists of six installations designed to provide visitors with refreshment areas characterized by elements of great scenic impact. The materials are banal: ice, snow, canvas, metal, candles and camping equipment. The project is intended as a reflection on natural space, which is re-created through temporary installations.

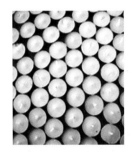

"Un-Volumetric Architecture"
Some notes on a new critical fulcrum
James Wines, President of SITE

> "De-architecture is a way of dissecting, shattering, dissolving, inverting and transforming certain fixed prejudices about buildings, in the interest of discovering revelations among the fragments."
> James Wines —(from "De-architecture" —Rizzoli International 1987)

The title of this book, "Un-volumetric Architecture," intrigued me from the moment I received an invitation to contribute a text. From my interpretation of the subject, it seemed to suggest a search for creative alternatives to the overly volumetric, shape-making obsessions that dominate international building design today. I view this as a promising goal for the twenty-first Century.

Most of the examples listed in this publication as "un-volumetric architecture" apply to structures with less density and mass —including, signage, territorial markers, bridges, canopies, public spaces, lighting elements and temporary interventions. In my view, the entire premise should go far beyond these categories and address the term's broader implications for design philosophy in the new millennium. By limiting the definition of un-volumetric architecture to the physical characteristics of certain structures, it risks underestimating the more conceptually progressive and environmentally responsible applications. As a critical tool, the term indicates a fertile point of departure for analyzing (and hopefully displacing) some of the sculptural excesses of formalist design. From a more practical perspective, it also provides a means of exposing the ecological irresponsibility associated with many contemporary architects' preference for such toxic building materials as titanium, aluminum, and a wide variety of petroleum-based products. And finally, it offers a premise for seeking alternatives to the kind of stylistic baggage, handed down from the early twentieth-century age of industry and technology, which has become increasingly inappropriate for signifying our present Age of Information and Ecology.

De-architecture, a book I wrote in 1985, was a significant precedent for the un-volumetric point of view and it pre-dated the design world's 1990s interest in *deconstruction*. This term was borrowed from the field of literary criticism and (incorrectly in my opinion) applied to a form of Neo-constructivist architecture, based on an aesthetic of discontinuity and fragmentation. My critical premise in *De-architecture* was the result of impatience with the design profession's endless recycling of Modernist, Cubist, and Constructivist influences. The thesis of the book proposed that, by constantly relying on these exhausted inspirational sources —particularly a persistent cribbing from Russian Constructivism— architecture had become resistant to the development of a new epochal sensibility and the need to change its aesthetic philosophy.

This gnawing issue of architects' indifference toward (or fear of) re-thinking their motivational premises appears to be an indication of the urgency of a design revolution in the new millennium. As I observed in *De-architecture*; "The language of architecture should now be more psychological than formal, more cosmic than rational, more informational than obscure, more provisional than stable, more indeterminate than resolved, more narrative than abstract... architecture of the future will convey a meaningful message if, and only if, architects are able to perceive it differently." Although I have changed some of my views since writing these words in the 1980s (mostly to focus on environmentally sustainable buildings), at that time I was simply making a case for revised thinking. My purpose reflected the mission of conceptual art, which meant shifting the emphasis in architecture from *physical* to *cerebral*.

As a result of its obligations to provide serviceable shelter, architecture is often seen by designers as constrained by its own earthbound physicality. At the opposite extreme in the arts, it is commonly accepted that a work of performance, video, or environmental art can readily step outside of formalist boundaries, by embracing notions of indeterminacy, ephemerality, and the absorption of information from a variety of sources.

The conceptual inhibitions of contemporary architecture are caused by an insufficient number of questions being asked and the misguided assumption that buildings are too burdened by function, budget, and gravity to explore any distracting ideas. This attitude represents a myopic detachment from the legacy of breakthroughs in the other arts and an unwillingness to experiment with new frames of reference. It is also the product of a century of architects' self-imposed limitations. There appears to be only one acceptable formula in the design process, drawn from that pivotal moment in history when the disdained nineteenth-century notion of *sculpture as a form of surface decoration on a building* was exchanged for the concept of *the whole edifice as a piece of sculpture in itself*. In contrast, the visual arts have been convulsed by many revolutions over the past one-hundred years —Post-impressionism, Cubism, Dadaism, Surrealism, Non-objectivism, Abstract Expressionism, Pop Art, Conceptualism, Minimalism, Earthworks, Performance Art, Video art, Trans-avant-garde, Hyper realism, and a plethora of lesser movements— while architecture has remained locked into to the same formalist commitments that were at the height of their relevance and creative fertility in the 1920s.

The self-proclaimed "socially responsible" cadre of architects explains its dismissal of art ideas as part of an obligation to respect the seriousness of the profession and the high costs of construction. These same designers also point out their ethical duty to avoid the risks of aesthetic frivolity (and I am sure this would include any considerations of an un-volumetric architecture). It is important to emphasize here that major changes in the arts have never been based on the limitations of pragmatism, an ease of execution, or a reduction in the cost of overhead —in fact, constraining circumstances often become the stimuli for innovation. As Picasso once observed; "Forcing yourself to use restricted means is the sort of restraint that liberates invention. It obliges you to make a kind of progress you can't even imagine in advance."

Advocating a similar economy of resources, Marcel Duchamp laid the foundations for conceptual art when he spoke of his work as "non-retinal" —announcing his lack of interest in the academic traditions of illusory representation, the seductive surfaces of Post-impressionist painting, and the crafted tactility of Cubist collage. His designation of non-retinal did not refer to invisibility— since, obviously, all forms of art (and especially architecture) are embodied in some kind of visible/tangible structure. Instead, Duchamp was staking out a claim for "art as the idea of art" —in other words, art to be experienced as more of a cerebral condition than a physical presence.

The conceptual artist, Joseph Kosuth, explained this attitudinal position in a seminal essay of the late 1960's, entitled *Art After Philosophy*. "Being an artist now means to question the nature of art. If one is questioning the nature of painting, one cannot be questioning the nature of art. Painting is a *kind* of art. If an artist accepts painting, he is accepting (and limited by) the traditional baggage that goes with it". Architects tend to avoid a comparable level of re-evaluation within their profession. This resistance to change —a form of conceptual inertia I call the "design mentality"— is antithetical to the quality of critical thinking exemplified by an artist like Duchamp, who once described his interrogatory process as: "I taught myself to contradict myself, in order to avoid conforming to my own taste."

It is no secret that most of contemporary disciples of latter day Modernism and Constructivism vehemently reject the notion that any shred of imagery in their architecture might be construed as referential or symbolic. Those perennial measures of design excellence, derived from the 1920's pioneers of abstract art, have ordained the virtues of formal relationships as preferable to what Robert Venturi once advocated as the "messy vitality" of popular culture and what I referred to in *De-architecture* as an open-ended design response to the psychological ambiguities of Jung's theory of the "collective unconscious." From the perspective of today's architectural rules of decorum, God forbid that an association with communicative content might pollute the sanctity of the form making/space making process. Architects like Peter Eisenman, Richard Meier, Dominique Perrault, Toyo Ito, Zaha Hadid, Daniel Liebskind and a host of other high design luminaries will jump through hoops to disclaim any connection with the untidy realms of allusion and narrative —and, even more vehemently, to distance themselves from the historical references and ornamental appendages identified with Post-modernism. What remains unacknowledged in all of this ideological posturing is the fact that the entire victory of formalist design was won over ninety years ago, during the earliest phases of the Modern Movement, when it became necessary to separate the progressive agendas of abstractionism from the decorative excesses of the Beaux Arts. To persist with these stale arguments in the contemporary world of information explosions and impending environmental disasters, has become quaintly anachronistic. In this regard, Neo-constructivism has become today's equivalent of a Beaux Arts redux.

Having started my professional life as a Constructivist-influenced sculptor —an artistic direction that I ultimately rejected in the late 1960s as archaic and derivative— my work in architecture, after 1970, has been based on the absorption of information from context. This approach has frequently included a questioning of design world values, by using the public's unconscious acceptance of buildings as the basis for a critical commentary on architecture's own rhetorical definitions. Especially in my work of the 1970's and 80's, this critique took the form of a shift of aesthetic intention away from formalist design, by proposing an architecture based on inversions of meaning and the inclusion of information from a variety of outside sources. During the 1970s and '80s (when I was working on the series of BEST Products Buildings) my conceptual viewpoint grew out of the observation that wall surfaces, interiors, landscape and public spaces can assimilate and reflect a broad range of subliminal messages that already exist in people's minds as a reaction to the built environment. I began treating the basic physical presence of architecture as a "filtering zone" for re-interpretation and as a wellspring for ideas that could be used to question many twentieth-century stylistic conventions. For example, rather than conceive of buildings as exercises in the making of *form, space and structure*, I shifted the emphasis to *idea, attitude and context*; or, (like conceptual art) to the notion of architecture as a dialogue in the mind. I observed that many archetypes —office towers, shopping centers, civic buildings, suburban homes, etc.— are ubiquitous and unseen objects of reflex identification in everyone's daily life. By taking advantage of this subliminal level of recognition, I found I could use buildings as the *subject matter* of art, as opposed to the objective of a conventional design process. In most cases, this meant retaining all of the familiar characteristics of routine recognition while adding or subtracting elements, which would then alter or question rhetorical meanings in architecture. For example, in a 1980 series of "illusion versus reality" Ghost Houses, I proposed converting the brick, stone, and shingle walls of a neighborhood of standard suburban bungalows into latex rubber, tin, lead, asphalt, Corten steel, and ferro-cement, while keeping the visual appearance of the original materials intact. As a result of this inversion, wood became lead, brick became rubber, stone became asphalt, and so forth. This rejection of the usual form-making process was typical of my earliest involvement with an un-volumetric sensibility. Needless-to-say, these explorations were dismissed by the architectural establishment as sacrilegious perversions during the 1970s (and, unfortunately, this work has been mostly misunderstood since that time).

Over the past decade, I have become increasingly involved with the environmental movement as it applies to green technology and the aesthetic relationships between buildings and their cultural/ecological surroundings. This shift of emphasis has also been controversial within conservative architectural circles. For example, I have frequently confronted the tendency of green design detractors to dismiss environmental concerns as peripheral (thus dumping all responsibility on the engineers) and disdain the use of garden spaces as nothing more than a form of pastoral sentimentality. This resistance to landscape and ecology opens up a number of intriguing issues concerning the relevance of the formalist opposition and the inclination of so many architects to marginalize the green movement. It is a rule of thumb in environmental circles that one tree means four people can breathe; so, just based on this health argument alone, it raises questions concerning why plants and trees in architecture are reduced to the status of mere décor, or eliminated altogether as superfluous intrusions. As mentioned earlier, part of the answer goes back to the earliest origins of Cubism and Constructivism, when the notion of architecture as a work of abstract sculpture became synonymous with good taste in design. Ironically, these stylistic references are usually dismissed by the art world as hopelessly old-fashioned —especially when they are resurrected as Henry Moore or Jean Arp-like organic form in the work of contemporary sculptors— while architects enthusiastically embrace these same influences as a source of cutting-edge emancipation.

The most blatant evidence of this reactionary aesthetic persuasion is very evident in design magazine presentations of prominent new buildings, where people and vegetation are conscientiously purged from photographs as a way of removing any distractions that might interfere with the readership's appreciation of some pristine formalist experience. This hermetic view of architecture has also contributed to the customary downgrading of landscape around buildings to nothing more than charm bracelets of lollypop trees and the relegation of public sculpture to "plop art" intrusions for people to lean on while waiting for a taxi.

Another curious aspect of architects' discomfort with conceptual and philosophical change is their confinement of computer technology to

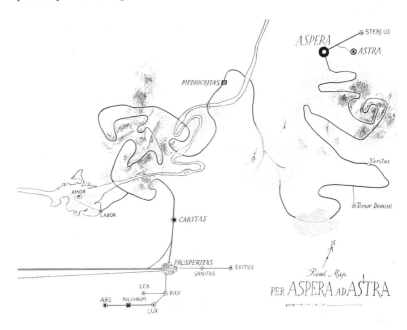

Saul Steinberg, image from "The labyrinth", Harper & Brother, Publisher, NY, 1954

churning out drawings of buildings that are nothing more than labyrinthine exercises in organic shape making and the usual manipulation of masonry, glass, steel, aluminum, and other manufactured materials. Sidetracked by these diversions, they overlook the fact that the digital phenomenon itself is the quintessential source of a new iconography —and especially applicable to the quest for an un-volumetric architecture. Just as the leading architects of the Industrial Age celebrated the weight and density of manufactured materials, why aren't their counterpart designers today mining the electronic revolution for fresh ideas? While mainstream designers seem to steadfastly avoid some of the most potent sources of imagery associated with the twenty-first, they also tend to see landscape as a violation of industrial design purity, social content as sentimental pabulum, sustainability concerns as a threat to formalist supremacy, and the computer as merely a useful tool to illustrate sculptural volumes that too often look as though they have been gleaned from a bad 1950's sculpture exhibition.

The present Age of Information and Ecology offers an incredibly fertile reservoir of ideas from science, popular culture and nature —cybernetics, virtual reality, mass media, biochemistry, hydrology, geology, and cosmology, just to mention a few. The architecture profession's failure to access these sources is indicative of its continuing conservatism and apparent lack of epochal awareness. As I observed at the conclusion of my recent book on *Green Architecture* (Taschen 2000): "Unlike the early Constructivists' works, which remained mostly unrealizable for the lack of computerized calculations and advanced construction technology, the CAD-equipped architect can easily describe and erect the most exotic configurations. Still, it seems oddly regressive to resurrect ideas from the 1920s, simply because they can be built today. And, finally, why have so few architects made the obvious conceptual and aesthetic connections between the integrated systems of the Internet and their ecological parallels in nature? These questions point to the need for developing a visionary *eco-digital* iconography in architecture. By incorporating ideas from both informational and ecological sources, it proposes the development of an imagery that echoes the mutable/evolutionary changes found in nature and the fluid/interactive flow of data through electronic communications. In spirit, this seems to indicate something more like trying to capture the intangibility of the wind passing through the trees than expressing the cumbersome mechanics of construction technology. It seems more like the quest for an *invisible or virtual architecture*, as opposed to celebrating the weight and density of industrial materials."

The early pioneering era of un-volumetric architecture began in the 1970s and 80s. It is most significantly represented by the work of innovative artists and architects like Gordon Matta-Clark, Robert Smithson, Gianni Pettena, Vito Acconci, Yves Klein, Christo, Claes Oldenburg, Nam June Paik, Alan Sonfist, Dennis Oppenheim, Robert Venturi, Ugo la Pietra, Franco Raggi, Gaetano Pesce, Peter Cook, and groups like Ant Farm, Archigram, Archizoom Super Studio, UFO, Haus Rucker, Onyx, and SITE. With few exceptions, most of the constructed projects during the early days of what was then called "Radical Architecture" fell into the category of installation art or temporary intervention. Also, the work was frequently manifested in the form of social/political/environmental commentary and served as a challenge to establishment design traditions. The value of this movement was credited at length in my book, *De-architecture*, as a means of using architecture itself as the critique of architecture.

In Michel Foucault's explorations concerning the equivocal nature of language, versus its use a tool for rational thinking, he cited the blurred edges separating reason and madness. In a similar way, architecture conceived as the questioning of architecture deals with various levels of ambivalence and challenges to the status quo. When applied to formalist design, this kind of critique – for example, ideas based on inversion and indeterminacy - can become the premise for using buildings as a source of psychic inquiry and as the means to achieve an expanded awareness of context.

Quite frankly, whether a new direction in architecture is called invisible or un-volumetric is not the primary concern. These terms merely represent a convenient way of describing the need for fundamental changes in the way architecture will be perceived and built in the new millennium. As mentioned earlier, it is an accepted premise that all buildings are embodied in a weighty physicality, constrained by economics, and indebted to construction technology. The main objective now is to shift the conceptual priorities from material to immaterial, from hermetic to absorptive, from abstract to informational, and from wasteful to green. This mission also refers to a breaking down of barriers that have traditionally separated art, buildings, landscape, and the greater social/ecological context. And, finally, there is an urgent need for architecture to renew its sources of content by tapping into a broader range of cultural, scientific, and environmental references that have been mostly overlooked during the past few decades.

Credits

Mariano Andreani
Archipro Architects
Lucien den Arend
Aldo Aymonino
Alejo Bague
Olivio Barbieri
David Barbour
Gianni Berengo Gardin
Helene Binet
Jan Bitter
John Buchan
Fritz Busam
Serge Demailly
Carine Demeter, syb'l pictures
EMBT
Shuhei Endo Architect Institude
Rosa Feliu
Alexander Felix
Ruth Meca Fernández
Luis Seixas Ferreira Alves
Luigi Filetici
Mark Fisher Studio Ltd
Fabio Fornasari
Franken Architekten,
Hayley Franklin
Yann Friedl
Mitsumasa Fujitsuka
Garofalo Architect
Alex Gaultier
Monika Gora
Roland Halbe
Michael Heinrich
Juan Miguel Hernandez Leon
Thrainn Hauksson
Tymothy Hursley
Lourdes Jansana
David Joseph, ShoP Architects
Nicholas Kane
Furudate Katsuaki
Kida Katsuhisa
Guido Keune
Katsuhisa Kida
Yoshiharu Kitajiama
Ira Koers
Steingrimur Kristinsson
Martinez Lapeña -Torres Arquitectos
Mark LaRocca

Albert K. S. Lim
Members of the Ciudad Abierta
and students
from our Schools of Architecture
Duccio Malagamba
Mitsuo Matsouka
David Mendelsohn / Zefa
Philippe Migeap
Neeser
Maurice Nio
Tomio Ohashi
Eamon O'Mahoney
Kas Oosterhuis
Chip Pankey
Richard Pare
Hans Pattist
Christian de Portzamparc
Pugh + Scarpa
Paul Van Rafelghem
Christian Richters
Piet Rook
Esther Rovira
Philippe Ruault
Armando Salas
Simone Scardovelli
Marco Scarpa
Sigurgeir Sigurjónsson
Sipe Architect
Societé des Autoroutes Paris-Rhin-
Rhône, Service de la Communication
Studio Acconci
Htsao Suzuki
Pierre Thibault
Jussi Tiainen, HUT photography
laboratory
Alan Ward
WEST 8 / Jeroen Mush
Bradley Wheeler
Beat Widmer
Nigel Young / Foster and Partners
Venturi, Scott Brown
and Associates
Andreas Vogler
Winfrid Zakowski
Giovanni Zanzi
Cino Zucchi
Gerald Zugmann